3 Steps to Your Best Job Ever!

Second Edition

Steven Steinfeld

Copyright © 2014 Steven Steinfeld
All rights reserved.

ISBN: 1478194065
ISBN 13: 9781478194064

Dedicated to Laura Sterkel

Table of Contents

Preface	VII
The 3 Steps	1
Step 1 - Discovery	3
Step 2 - Preparation	8
Step 3 - Action	11
New Grad and Hired	13
6 Ways to a Job Interview	23
Developing Your Value Statement	27
Effective Resumes	33
Compelling Cover Letters	49
Strategic Networking	55
LinkedIn and Other Social Media	69
The Power of the Informational Interview	81
Mastering Job Interviews	99
Non-Profit Work	141
Volunteer Strategically	145
Working with 3rd Parties and References	147
Negotiating Like a Pro	153
Long-term Unemployment	157
Job Search from the Inside Out	163
About the Author	167

Preface

"Luck is what happens when preparation meets opportunity."

– Seneca, Roman Philosopher

This second edition of *3 Steps to Your Best Job Ever* contains all of the practical and proven strategies, tactics and tips from the first edition—plus valuable new insights from my clients, readers, and workshop attendees. It not only tells you **WHAT** to do and **WHY** — but also shows you exactly **HOW** to do it with easy to modify examples.

Despite some improvement in the overall economy over the last few years, job hunting continues to be challenging for the majority of professionals. If you have not been in a job search recently, you may be surprised to know that up to 80% of jobs are never posted, fewer than 25% of posted jobs are filled by an outside candidate, and it's no longer unusual for a company to receive thousands of resumes in response to a single posting.

Everything you need to know to be a successful job seeker is contained in this book. If you are in a particularly negative or discouraged state of mind, you might want to start by reading the last chapter of the book titled "Job Search from the Inside Out." Otherwise, please read it carefully from the beginning unless you have an immediate need such as a resume update or impending interview. In order to keep you engaged, I have done my best to keep the information organized, simple and sometimes entertaining.

I often meet with job seekers who have received conflicting or just plan terrible advice from well-meaning friends and family members, and sometimes even from job counsellors still following antiquated job search methods. This can create a lot of confusion. I strongly believe that to have a successful job search you are best served by putting your faith in a single source (for example, this book).

Please note that gender pronouns and terms such as "job search," "job searching," "job hunter," job seeker," and "in transition," are used interchangeably. Throughout your reading, please focus on content rather than the specific choice of words or industry or specific job examples. **This book is intended for ALL young, mid-career and long term unemployed professionals facing a challenging job search, including soon to be graduates and recent grads.**

The 3 Steps

"I Never Did a Day's Work in My Life. It was All Fun!"
— Thomas Edison

I am about to introduce you to the 3 steps — **Discovery, Preparation and Action** — that will give you the basic structure you will need to follow to separate yourself from other job candidates. Discovery will help you identify the best job opportunities. Preparation will show you how to develop the tools necessary to effectively tell your story, and Action will teach you how to engage with people who can refer, recommend or hire you.

The successful use of the 3 steps requires that you:

- Come to understand the value of your strengths (soft skills) and relationships. Extensive experience, a track record of success, an excellent education and/or a good technical skill set will not guarantee you a job
- Select realistic jobs to pursue for which you have genuine enthusiasm and the tools (knowledge, experience, strengths, skills) to succeed

- Be proactive (the meek may inherit the earth but they are terrible at job search)

- Go the extra mile (this leg of the race is usually not very crowded)

- Put aside the traditional ideas of how a job search should be conducted.

- Understand that job search is a marketing and sales campaign that requires the help and support of others to get your message out to a wide audience.

- Go directly to the hiring manager whenever possible, bypassing HR

- Stay active, confident, positive and focused

The 3 STEPS

 Discovery

 Preparation

 Action

- Inventory Your Interests, Strengths, and Values—Combine with Your Skills, Knowledge, Experience
- Brainstorm, Research, and Evaluate Realistic Opportunities
- Focus on One or Two Positions and a List of Target Companies
- Develop Your Resume, Cover Letter, and LinkedIn Profile
- Get Organized with Written Goals and Networking Plans
- Network into Target Companies with Informational Interviews
- Master Job Interviews
- Negotiate the Final Offer

THE 3 STEPS

Step 1 – Discovery

Before continuing your job search, you are strongly advised to spend time identifying opportunities that are well suited to your skills, education, training, and experience—and also to your personality, interests, strengths and values. **I call each of these opportunities, your *right* job.** Often the challenge lies not only in finding the *right* jobs, but in finding the *right* organizations, with opportunity for learning and advancement, and the *right* culture.

Think you're too old or financially strapped to pursue the *right* job? You may not only be better prepared than you think, but doing so is often the key to success. **You will be a much stronger candidate if you have genuine enthusiasm for the jobs and organizations you are targeting, since you will be much more likely to bring focus, energy and confidence into your job search efforts.**

Begin your job search with the DISCOVERY step described below. It will help you save valuable time by determining which jobs and organizations you should pursue, and will also help you to avoid investing in additional education, training or certifications that may be of little value.

Even if you think you are on the right path, you should spend a little time validating your path in a Discovery step. There are over 400 broad professional job classifications and over 800 detailed professional job classifications, many of which you have probably not considered. There are also millions of employers in the U.S., including over 18,000 with more than 500 employees — each with a somewhat unique culture.

Start the Discovery step by taking an inventory of your strengths, sometimes called "soft skills." These are different from ("hard") skills such as MS Office that are learned through training). Strengths refer to talents that have been developed from a young age and cannot be easily taught. For example, it would be very difficult to train someone to be creative or detail oriented or a great problem solver. As discussed at length in the chapter titled *Mastering Job Interviews,* **your unique combination of strengths is** often more important than your knowledge, experience or skills in determining whether or not you will be offered the job.

Your strengths likely include several of the following, and maybe some others not listed here:

- Adaptable
- Creative
- High Energy
- Detail Oriented
- Self-Motivated
- Team Player
- Leader
- Planner
- Verbal and/or Written Communicator
- Problem Solver (Critical Thinker)
- Accountable
- Versatile
- Fast Learner
- Results Oriented
- Dependable
- Strategic Thinker
- Disciplined
- Dedicated
- Hard-Working
- Task-Oriented

Your strengths, along with your interests and work values, will also determine the companies where you will be most successful. If the position is a good match with your strengths and interests, you are likely to be more engaged in the work and therefore much more likely to do an outstanding job. On the other side, when a job does not work out, it is usually because of a problem fitting into the culture rather than a problem with the work itself. For example, if a team oriented culture is important to you, there is a good chance that you will not be happy or fully engaged at a company that does not particularly value teamwork.

You can use assessment tools such as The Myers-Briggs Type Indicator (MBTI), StrengthsFinder 2.0, or the Strong Interest Inventory to give you concrete ways to name and categorize your strengths even if you generally know what they are. But should you decide not to use formal assessment tools, you can still get some understanding of your interests and strengths from the simple exercise below.

Answer the Following Questions About Your Interests and Strengths

- What do I enjoy doing most outside of work?
- What are my greatest work accomplishments (including volunteer work)?
- Which job has helped me grow the most? How?
- What did I enjoy doing best at my most recent job? What did I like least?
- What do I consider, or have others mentioned, to be my personal and professional strengths?
- What combination of strengths, skills, and knowledge makes me valuable, special or unique?
- When have I been amazed, absorbed, inspired or excited by my work?
- If I could choose my next job or career without monetary concerns, what would I do?

Brainstorm Potential Opportunities

Assemble some key words from your formal and/or informal assessments and put those words into job search engine www.indeed.com along with some related job and industry descriptors (e.g., "innovative" "teamwork" "strategic" "sales" "communication skills" "software"). It doesn't matter if the results that come up are in your local area or a different geography. What you are trying to accomplish is identifying potential jobs that mesh well with your interests, strengths, skills, experience, knowledge, and values. Indeed.com is an aggregator of job postings, so you don't need to go to several job search engines to accomplish the same result.

Set up alerts with keywords on indeed.com to be automatically notified about job postings that meet your criteria, and keep the alerts with the most relevant results active during your entire job search.

Identify job descriptions from the results that are a potential fit, and get you excited.

How to Evaluate Your Match to a Job Posting

> Assess the most interesting job postings by highlighting the job requirements and job responsibilities within the posting in 3 different colors:
> **GREEN, YELLOW and RED.**
> **Be sure to highlight every line in the posting.**
> **GREEN:** A great fit/This attracts me to the job/I am very confident and have hands-on experience
> **YELLOW:** Does not apply to me/I haven't done this before/ I am less than 100% confident
> **RED:** This is a potential turn-off or deal breaker

You can also mark each Skills related bullet point on the job description with an "H" for "Hard Skills" and an "S" for "Soft Skills." This will give you an idea of the mix of those skills required and preferred by the employer.

THE 3 STEPS

Note the relative location of each job requirement, job responsibility, and skill listed. The ones that are most important to the company will be listed near the top.

If you match at least 80% of the requirements in GREEN (with no RED), and also match well with the soft and hard skills near the top of the skills section; the opportunity should be investigated further.

If you are really excited about the job, but have a significant education or knowledge gap that makes that opportunity unrealistic right now, you may want to consider investing in closing that gap by taking additional classes or by getting hands-on training so that you can pursue a similar opportunity in the future. If the job is a great fit, but there is one item in red, look for a similar job posting without that one show stopper.

If you see a job that is less than an 80% match, but you are very interested in the organization, check the company's job board for positions that may be a better match. **You will sometimes find that you are much more qualified for a job one step below the job advertised.**

Once you have selected jobs to investigate, you will want to set up one or more informational interviews for each one since there is no easier way to assess a job than by talking to someone who has been working at that job. See the chapter titled *The Power of the Informational Interview* for how to arrange and conduct these important meetings during the Discovery step.

Before leaving the DISCOVERY step, make a preliminary list of jobs, industries and companies to investigate.

You will know for sure that you are on track to getting the *right* job when you start getting in-person job interviews. Sometimes job seekers come in second or third out of hundreds of candidates in the competition for their targeted job, but become frustrated and totally change course. Don't fall into this trap! Continue to hone your job searching skills, and you will jump to number one.

If you must take something less than your *right* job to meet your financial obligations, look at the job as transitional and keep working toward better options.

Step 2 – Preparation

You may know that story of the two lumberjacks that entered a contest to see who could fell a giant tree more quickly, a young and very strong lumberjack and a much older and experienced one. While the younger lumberjack chopped and sawed furiously without pause, he noticed that the older lumberjack was taking breaks to sit down. But when they came to the end of the contest, the older lumberjack had won. "I don't get it, the younger lumberjack said to the older one. While I never took a break, I noticed that you sat down to rest a few times." "Oh, I wasn't resting," the older lumberjack replied. I was sharpening my tools."

The second step in your job search, PREPARATION, refers to getting your job search tools organized and sharpened. Failure to take the necessary time to do so will likely derail you job search efforts. During this step, you will need to have your value statement, resume, cover letter, and LinkedIn profile sharpened more than once (we discuss each of these in some detail in future chapters), but start by getting organized with written goals and your calendar. **The formats and methods that you use to get organized do not matter as long as you write everything down.** You might use a spreadsheet, phone app, or even a paper list held by a magnet on your refrigerator.

Your job search goals and plans are best set at the beginning of each week, and should contain a variety of activities and approaches including: social networking, phone calls, responses to job postings, networking events (especially those connected to alumni organizations, industry conferences, and professional associations), external recruiters, and informational interviews. Also include related job search activities such as industry and company research. Your goals should be S-M-A-R-T. This stands for Specific, Measurable, Achievable, Realistic, and Timely.

Set goals and plans for no more than two related jobs. If you have two (e.g., financial analyst and accountant), you don't need to spend an equal amount of time on each one. For example, you might spend 80% of your time on activities relevant to your first choice target job, and 20% on activities relevant to your second choice. Of course, some activities (e.g., attending a networking event) might span both your first and second choice targeted jobs. **Some weeks will be more successful than others, but each week will be more productive with written goals than without them.**

My Job Search Goals	Week of:
My First Job Choice: Accountant	My Second Job Choice: Financial Analyst
To Accomplish This Week	To Accomplish This Week
1- 2- 3- 4-	1- 2-
What I Actually Accomplished	What I Actually Accomplished
1- 3- 4-	1- 2-

At the end of the week, ask yourself the following four questions before setting your goals for the next week:

1. Have I accomplished all of my goals for the week? If not, why not?

2. What's been working?

3. What has not been working?

4. What do I need to do more of? Less of? Change or improve?

In addition to your written goals, you will need a target prospect log. The following are some of the things you may want to keep track of in this log:

- **Information on your target companies.** Select 10 or 20 companies that hire people like you, then research the company and log the information from your research. This information may include: industry, location, target position, referral contact, the date you submitted your resume and cover letter, opportunity status (e.g., hot, cold), and additional comments.

- **Contact information for people you plan to connect with at target companies.** Include the date that you plan to contact and follow-up with each person, including your method of contact (e.g., email, phone, LinkedIn).

In addition to contacts at target companies, you should also list and track contacts that might be able to provide you with new information or advice.

Spend most of your available time researching companies and potential opportunities, establishing potentially valuable relationships, and setting informational interviews.

At the end of each week, measure and compare your results (new contacts made, contacts added to LinkedIn, number of informational interviews, resume submissions leading to job interviews, and hours spent on each activity).

Before leaving the PREPARATION step, ask yourself the following questions:

> - Are my job search goals clear and in writing?
>
> - Have I created easy to use tools to keep track of my weekly goals and networking plans?
>
> - Have I developed a compelling value statement, and do I practice it frequently? (See the chapter titled *Developing Your Value Statement*).
>
> - Does my resume get across what I need to highlight for the specific job(s) I am targeting? (See the chapter titled *Effective Resumes*).

Step 3 – Action

Finally, but not necessarily after a long time, you will enter the ACTION step. In this step, you will concentrate on executing your plan, and also take daily and weekly actions to measure, assess and refine your results.

When you see a job posting of great interest and viability (lots of Green, little Yellow, and no Red), quickly locate and meet with an employee or ally of the hiring manager* who might be willing to personally bring your resume forward within the company (see the chapter titled *The Power of the Informational Interview* for how to arrange and conduct these interviews).

*When I use the term "hiring manager," I am always referring to the individual responsible for making a particular hiring decision, often the future employee's supervisor, not the HR person who may formally present the job offer.

If you cannot get an informational interview with someone who can hand deliver your resume within two weeks from the job posting, send your resume and cover letter directly to the hiring manager, but keep trying to set up informational interviews.

If you cannot identify the hiring manager or connect with an employee or other ally of the hiring manager within 3 weeks from the job posting, send your resume and cover letter to a specific HR professional within the company (e.g., the VP or Director), and continue to keep trying to set up informational interviews.

See the chapter titled *Effective Resumes* for tips on how to identify and contact hiring managers and other employees, including HR professionals.

While in the ACTION step, continually ask yourself the following questions:

- Have I thoroughly identified and researched my target industries, organizations, jobs, and potential hiring managers?
- Am I bringing quality and professionalism to everything I do? This includes a professional email address and a professional voice mail message on your cell phone.
- If I am planning to send my resume and cover letter, have I done everything possible to identify the names and contact information of hiring managers?
- Am I putting enough time into my job search efforts?
- Am I using the tools I created in the preparation step to stay organized?
- **What do I offer to each job and company I am pursuing?**
- **What does each job and company offer me?**
- **Am I setting myself apart from other candidates?**
- Do I need professional help?

Please note that the 3 steps are not mutually exclusive and are sometimes overlapping. For example, the ACTION step will always take you back to PREPARATION, and possibly back to DISCOVERY.

New Grad and Hired

"The future depends on what we do in the present"
— Mahatma Gandhi

This chapter assumes that you are a young recent graduate or a student nearing graduation. If you have already been out of school and working for a number of years, you can skip this chapter.

Please note that the information in all chapters of this book are for students and recent grads with some obvious, and only a few notable, exceptions. For example, you may have a 7th way to a job interview by virtue of meeting with an on-campus recruiter, and in most cases should have a one-page resume with your Education section at the top directly under your summary statement as noted in the chapter titled "Effective Resumes."

Keys to Building a Career in Your 20's

Gain Relevant Experience

Don't expect to walk into your dream job right from college or grad school. Just like your first house is not likely to be a mansion, your first real job will be the equivalent of a starter home, and a stepping stone to that mansion in the future. Gaining experience, and a better understanding of your career options, is what you can expect from that first job out of school—anything else is a bonus.

It's critical that you show a history of relevant career experience as soon as possible. Fortunately, this can include part-time, temporary, volunteer and summer work in addition to internships (the more, the merrier), especially paid internships which have been shown to be a major precursor to job offers. Even if it appears difficult to show relevance (your only work history is working at a country club or summer camp), you will be able to bring out some important work strengths such as work ethic, leadership, customer focus, and achievement. Below are resume bullets from two students who sold vacuums during summer vacation. Which one might you hire

Student 1: Sold vacuums door-to-door during the summer.

Student 2: Sold 102 vacuums door-to-door. By working overtime, became one of the youngest salespeople ever to sell over 100 vacuums during the company's summer season.

Follow Your Passion

While you need to balance idealism with realism, assuming you do not have severely limiting financial or family obligations—there will never be a better time to see how far your interests and passion can take you. Don't be dissuaded by well-meaning family members who value safety and security. Make it known that you are following your passion in your networking, resume, cover letters, and interviewing. People who follow their passion are much more engaged in their work, and are often both happy and successful.

Develop Your Strengths

Strengths reflect your interests and talents (writing, public speaking, problem solving) that have been developed from a young age. They are different than skills that are training related (spreadsheet development). Look for jobs that utilize your strengths, and help develop them. For example, if you are persuasive, think strategically, and enjoy working with people in a challenging environment, you might consider an entry level sales job. Over time, that job may lead to sales management or even executive management.

Build Your Professional Network

Use social networking to build your network, and meet in person with as many contacts as possible. Start NOW and NEVER STOP!

Handle Age Stereotypes

Younger workers tend to be seen with the following strengths or advantages:
- Physically able, healthy
- Easy to supervise
- Flexibility
- Lower salary expectations
- Technology and social networking savvy
- Creativity
- High energy

- Motivated to take initiative
- Willingness to endure long hours
- Ability to multi-task

However, when competing against older, more seasoned workers, they may be seen as lacking the following:

- Industry knowledge
- Reasoning and planning skills
- Relationship building skills
- Achievements (awards)
- Tested personal strengths (resilience, integrity)
- Professionalism
- Strategic thinking
- Problem solving ability
- Communication skills
- Leadership ability
- Organizational skills
- An excellent work ethic
- Experience
- Reliability
- Loyalty
- Maturity
- Stability

In addition to exhibiting the characteristics that are expected, a younger worker should concentrate on exhibiting the positive characteristics typically associated with older workers.

Focus on Large Companies or Start-Ups

Large companies will invest in developing your skills and knowledge, especially if you show technical competence. However, if you are exceptionally entrepreneurial or technically gifted, or both, you might want to join a start-up where you will be given a high degree of responsibility immediately.

Keep Advanced Degrees in Perspective

While advanced degrees (e.g., MA/MS, JD, and MBA) can be instrumental in getting you a better job opportunity now, and positively influence your future opportunities for advancement, they are much more common than they used to be. An advanced degree is not a guaranteed ticket to a great job, and talking about it too much can give the impression of entitlement, particularly when talking to an older hiring manager who worked his way up without one.

Be Sensitive to Generational Differences

Today's recent graduates expect to be treated more as an equal than past generations. This can come into conflict with older hiring managers and HR people who grew up in a more top down environment who expect some deference for their experience and accomplishments. Always show gratitude for the opportunity to learn and grow.

Investigate the Culture of the Organization

You will be much happier and will survive much longer at an organization that values participation, teamwork, informality, and fun.

Follow Up

When I ask recent graduates why they don't follow up, answers include, "They should be contacting me," and "I'd rather postpone the bad news." Following up is critical, and shows that you care. If you are not following up, you may want to question if you are pursuing the right job.

Understand Traditional Business Etiquette

A job interview requires formal business dress and professionalism. If in doubt, get advice from a knowledgeable source.

Don't Rush Into a Job

Even though you may have some heavy student loans, need to finance your apartment, or get your parents off your back, carefully think through whether the job fits with your short and long-term plans before accepting it.

Q. Are there jobs for liberal arts graduates in today's high tech business world?
A. Of course. A degree in liberal arts is highly respected by many companies in the business world for the critical analysis, problem solving, creativity, and logical reasoning they bring. Pick a major that you love, and focus on getting multiple internships that match your career goals—but have a clear career strategy since many jobs for liberal arts majors require an advanced degree.

Q. How can best take advantage of a career or job fair?
A. Go to the event with the intention of gathering information about companies as you would in informational interviews. Get a list of companies coming to the fair, and research ones of particular interest before you go, practice your value statement, and prepare some questions that you will want answered. For example, you may want to ask questions such as "What is the standard hiring process?" or "What do they look for in a

candidate?" In addition, you will want to remember to ask for the name of the appropriate hiring manager.

Here are some helpful career and job fair tips:

- Always dress professionally.

- A job fair can also be looked as providing mini-interview opportunities, so prepare to answer the same basic questions you might be asked at a job interview.

- Bring notes from your company research and a list of 3 questions to ask each representative.

- Get maximum time with company representatives by being one of the first to arrive.

- Practice your approach with companies of lesser interest before approaching your "top" companies.

- Start and end your conversation with company representatives with a friendly smile, a firm handshake, direct eye contact, energy, and a confident posture with your shoulders back.

- Make sure you take each representative's business card and company literature.

- Take notes on how to follow up on a small pad or your phone right after leaving each conversation.

- Go to job fairs at other schools and venues in your area in addition to your own. Find them at www.natonalcareerfairs.com.

Q. Can my alumni career services office and association help?
A. Check with your career services office for services they provide to alumni (e.g., resume and cover letter reviews). Even if you don't attend alumni

events, read the alumni newsletter and magazine carefully for networking and career opportunities.

Q. Will I be able to get a good job without graduating from a top school or without outstanding grades?
A. Either of those will help you get interviews, but your school's reputation and a high GPA will not guarantee you a great job. Beyond reputation and academic success, employers today are looking for resumes that include a work history, extracurricular achievements, leadership activities, community service, and/or specific technical skills.

Q. How important are internships?
A. An internship can be full or part-time, and paid or unpaid depending on the employer and the career field. You will enhance your job prospects greatly if you can get a paid internship—but even if you are not paid; an internship offers the benefit of hands-on-learning and the potential to give you an edge over students without internships.

An internship can also provide you with important networking introductions and references needed to identify and land a job after graduation; and you may even be lucky enough to be mentored by executives, have the opportunity to input ideas to a project team, or present to a group of senior-level managers. If you cannot get a traditional internship, consider alternatives in order to gain experience. For example, if you are a finance student, try for a part-time job at a financial advisor's office.

Once you land that internship, think of the internship as a several-week long interview, and work very hard to demonstrate that you have the strengths and skills that will make you a valuable addition to the company when you finish school. However, before you accept any internship, make sure that you will have significant job duties that result in achievement and learning.

Even after graduation, you may want to take advantage of an internship. There is a common misconception that internships are only for college students. Internships are for anyone who has some knowledge in his field but lacks the relevant hands-on experience that employers want to see before they offer a regular full time position.

Job Search is Similar to Dating

Before reading on, it may be helpful to think of an effective job search in the same way you might think about dating. You might go to a party (*networking event*) or on an online dating service, but either way you will want to give some thought in advance about how you want to be perceived. What are you going to say about yourself that it compelling to the point that she will want to know more about you (*your value statement*). If there is interest, she will want to know about your background including your school and work history (*your resume*), and you will want to add some compelling information that may not be obvious (*your cover letter*). If it goes well, she will encourage a first date (*initial interview*). She will likely investigate you on Facebook and LinkedIn (*for your brand*), and maybe do a Google search on your name before the date. On the date, additional basic and behavioral questions will be asked. The more experience you have had with dating (*interviewing*), the more likely that you will have developed effective answers. At the end of the date you will want to get some indication of whether there will be a second date (*next steps*). You will probably follow up to express how much you enjoyed the date and are looking forward to the next date (thank you note). You will introduce her to some of your friends (*for recommendations*), and she will introduce you to some of her friends (*for reinforcement*). You both think about whether marriage (*full time position*) might work, and compare each other to exes or other singles you know (*the decision process*). Finally, after you discuss children and where to live (*negotiation*), you decide to ask her to get married (*job offer*). Of course, if you were too eager to get married, you might have overlooked some negatives in the situation, and the marriage may end in a painful separation. This is why it is critical to only seek Ms R*ight* (*the job*) and the R*ight* family (*the organization*) from the start.

6 Ways to a Job Interview

"There are many ways of going forward, but only one way of standing still"

— Franklin D. Roosevelt

One job search misconception that you might have is that the only way to get a job interview is to send your resume to a company in response to a job posting. **This chapter is intended to help you understand that there are at least six ways, and that they are not equally effective or successful in getting you the interview or priority consideration.**

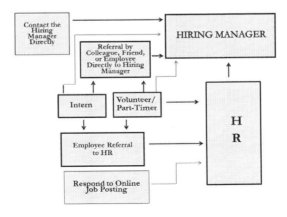

3 STEPS TO YOUR BEST JOB EVER!

1. The most effective way to get a job interview is to connect with a "hiring manager"* directly or indirectly with a strong referral and/or recommendation from an employee, friend or colleague of that hiring manager. The informational interview is a great way to get this kind of referral and recommendation (See the chapter titled *The Power of the Informational Interview*). A job offer is not guaranteed, but the interview is assured.

2. One of the next best ways to get a job interview is through an employee in good standing referral to the HR department, even without a strong recommendation. HR professionals assume that an employee will not bring forward a candidate for consideration less qualified than the employee doing the referring, and will often feel an obligation to give the employee's candidate serious consideration. Companies have also found that job candidates who are recommended by valued employees tend to perform better, stay longer and integrate faster. This is why resumes submitted by an employee get special attention as compared to resumes submitted online.

3. You may look upon internships as being only for young students, but it is actually another way for professionals in many occupations to get an offer for a full time position, particularly in a career change situation where the hiring manager (or a close colleague of the hiring manager) has a chance to observe your skills and strengths first hand.

4. Volunteering, even for a few hours per week on a regular basis, is a very good way to get the attention of a hiring manager or an employee who might bring you to the attention of a hiring manager or the HR department. (See the chapter titled *Volunteer Strategically*).

5. Another way that you can improve your chances of landing an interview and job offer requires going around HR to get to the hiring manager with your resume directly—**whether or not there is a job posting.** HR professionals often follow a relatively slow process, and may not fully understand the skills and strengths desired by the hiring manager. The hiring manager, on the other hand, is mainly concerned about finding the right candidate as quickly as possible, even if it means bending company policy and procedure. If the timing is good, and you engage him directly with the ability to present yourself as an exceptional candidate, there is a good chance that he will arrange for you to be interviewed. As with the five ways above, this approach will bring your resume priority. **It may be difficult for you to accept the idea that you should avoid the official HR application process, but you will often dramatically increase your odds of success if you do.**

6. The sixth and least successful path to landing an interview is submitting your resume online to HR (with or without a cover letter). One reason is that you are "unknown" and there is a good chance that the hiring manager and HR will find enough "known" candidates using the other approaches already discussed before seriously considering online candidates. If you only take the online approach, it can result in a very long and frustrating job search and/or a job that is less satisfying than one you might have landed if you had used one of the other approaches.

This book will not only explain how to utilize the five best ways to get a job interview, but will even increase your chances of successfully using the online method.

Developing Your Value Statement

"Your brand is what people say about you when you're not in the room"

— Jeff Bezos, Founder of Amazon

If I gave you 30 seconds to tell me why someone should hire you, would you be able to give me a clear, confident, and compelling answer?

When someone asks, "What do you do?" or, "Tell me about yourself," you should be hearing, "What do you do best professionally?" and "What value do you bring to a particular type of organization or client?" Respond with an answer that is prepared, but sounds casual and genuine. If the person asking the question can help your job search, the answer you give may be critical.

Everyone has experience with brands. A brand conveys a promise of performance and is what you think of when you see a particular logo. Think about everything conveyed in Coca-Cola's logo or BMW's brand promotion as the "ultimate driving machine." When someone leaves a conversation with you, he should have a similarly memorable image—your professional brand, "Steven Steinfeld? He's a popular and respected job search author, speaker and coach."

Your goal during job hunting should be to grab the listener's attention, and create interest in knowing more about how your proven value can be put to use by a specific organization. In job search coaching, we often call the expression of your brand, your "value statement." A value statement, often referred to as an "elevator pitch," should be a powerful promise of performance that can be delivered in a short amount of time, sometimes as little as thirty seconds. It should sound confident, unscripted, and unrehearsed—not a desperate plea for help.

Even if you do your best to develop your personal brand, it's other people who ultimately determine your brand. If you want to know more about your brand as it exists today, ask your former colleagues what characteristics they think of when they think of you. This should help you develop a value statement that's in tune with your real strengths.

If you are lucky enough to have a passion for a certain type of work, don't settle for anything less, but remain flexible as to your job responsibilities and job title. Make it known that you are following your passion in your value statement (and in your networking, resume, cover letters, and interviewing). Job candidates who follow their passion are more likely to be recommended and hired since people assume that job seekers who are following their passion will work especially hard and be more successful in their careers.

Need help getting started? Write down a few things that set you apart from other people who do what you do. Then add one or more significant results you are confident you can deliver. Once done, design a simple statement to get your main point or two across.

Your value statement should present you as a specialist who can help a specific type of employer or client with an immediate challenge, rather than a generalist since generalists don't get hired as often. **Avoid talking too much about your experience — concentrate instead on getting across what you can deliver going forward.**

DEVELOPING YOUR VALUE STATEMENT

Don't be afraid to brag, but if you have a problem talking about yourself in superlatives, such as "I am a job search coaching genius," say, "Other people often tell me that I am a job search coaching genius."

You can start crafting your value statement with one of the brief exercises below. In the first example, the respondent is a telecommunications equipment salesperson. Think of the difference in impact if he answered the query, "What do you do?" by simply saying, "I'm in sales."

SAMPLE VALUE STATEMENT WORKSHEET

My Career Focus	I sell complex networking solution to wireless companies.
Highlight strengths, skills, or knowledge that have allowed you to successfully help a company or set of individuals	I've had a successful career because I've developed technical and engineering knowledge in addition to executive level sales skills.
Explain the work you are pursuing or the types of organizations that are your focus	I'm currently investigating opportunities at European equipment suppliers, but also looking at U.S. start-ups.
Ask for informational interview referrals	If you know anyone who might give me some company information or advice, I would appreciate it very much.

MY VALUE STATEMENT WORKSHEET

My Career Focus	
Highlight strengths, skills, or knowledge that have allowed you to successfully help a company or set of individuals	
Explain the work you are pursuing or the types of organizations that are your focus	
Ask for informational interview referrals	

Now practice your value statement. When ready, test it by imagining that you enter an elevator alone with the person who can hire you. You have as little as thirty seconds to deliver your "elevator pitch" before reaching the ground level. Are you comfortable with what you are going to say? Do you sound conversational? Speak slowly and clearly when delivering your value statement. 30 seconds is a lot longer than you might think. If you watch a politician give a speech, notice that he uses dramatic pauses in between key words or sentences. You should do the same with your value statement. Give the listener time to reflect on what you are saying.

One good way to enhance your practice is to record yourself on your smart phone and play it back to see if you sound confident and to check for relevance, lack of repetition and clarity.

DEVELOPING YOUR VALUE STATEMENT

In real world situations, you will have much more than 30 seconds, and you will often need to weave your value statement into the conversation in bits and pieces. You should also tailor you statement to the person. For example, if you are interested in a job in marketing, you would choose different words when speaking to a marketing professional than you would to someone who knows little or nothing about marketing. If you stay focused, you should be able to get across everything you want to say (and ask) before the conversation ends.

In addition to the spoken value statement you need for networking and interviewing, you will also want to use modified, sometimes more formal, written versions of your value statement at the top of your resume, and within your cover letter and LinkedIn profile. Any time you improve your value statement, update the three written versions. In any event, you should continually refine all four, and tailor each one for different situations and opportunities.

Effective Resumes

"If you call failures experiments, you can put them in your resume and claim them as achievements."

— Mason Cooley, American Aphorist

Even if you come to an employer with a strong recommendation, a resume that is not well written can stand between you and a job offer.

Write your resume yourself with the help of the information in this chapter. If you give it to someone to edit, be sure that you are comfortable with every word being used, and it sounds like you wrote it yourself. If you are considering hiring a resume service, only do so if absolutely necessary, and only work with someone with an impeccable reputation who is willing to spend considerable time working closely with you for a reasonable cost.

I have seen very few resumes that could not be improved dramatically. One of the main reasons is that job seekers either do not get their resumes read by someone knowledgeable or they show it to ten "experts"—in which case you may get ten conflicting opinions on how to improve it.

This chapter lays out the best advice that I have gathered from seasoned career consultants, coaches and HR professionals, and the results of my own clients' experiences. This does not, however, mean that you should not show your resume to people whose opinions you value, preferably those in your same profession. It's critically important that you see your resume from the point of view of the reader.

Q. How many pages should my resume be?

A. If you are a student or recent graduate, your resume should be contained to one-page unless you have an unusually high number of relevant internships or jobs and extra-curricular activities to fill at least 1 ½ pages. For most professionals, it should be two pages. I have seen many two-page resumes that have been jammed into a single page using extra small font based on the misguided notion that a resume should not exceed one page. A one-page resume can be appropriate for a professional re-entering the workforce after a large gap or a job seeker changing careers with little relevant experience, but it would be better to work hard to make your two-page resume relevant. Three page resumes should be avoided by most job seekers, but I find that they can work well for very senior executives with a long track record of success, a consulting professional, or when a Curriculum Vitae (CV) is required in a legal, academic, or scientific field. A CV, as opposed to a resume, includes a detailed account of academic, public speaking, patents, publications, and research.

Q. What are the keys to an effective resume?

A. An effective resume needs to be easy to read, compelling, relevant, and contain measurable accomplishments.

Easy to read

Take out all unnecessary words, and put yourself into the position of the reader. Will he get an idea of your potential value in as little as six seconds (and no more than 20 seconds)? This is all the time that an HR professional may take (only looking at your last job title, start and end dates, and education). A hiring manager who has the incentive to read your resume by virtue of a personal recommendation may take longer, but probably still less than a minute. Easy readability is one reason to avoid functional resumes (another reason is that you may be seen as trying to hide gaps in your job history). Functional resumes list your skills in clusters rather than in chronological order, so they take more time to read and decipher. The same is true for "creative" resumes other than for professionals in especially creative professions such as graphic arts. You can follow the format in this chapter, use a professional resume template found at office.microsoft.com, or select a format that has been successful for a recent job hunter within your profession. Include getting copies of successful resumes as one of your networking goals.

Compelling at the Top

I am referring to the top of your resume which is critical since it may be the only part of your resume that may fully capture the attention of the reader. The format that I prefer is one in which you have a headline under your name that very specifically announces the job for which you are qualified (COMPLIANCE MANAGER - HEALTH CARE). Even though I believe that you should be narrowly targeting a job, the name of that position will fluctuate from organization to organization, so you will need to modify the headline to be in tune with the title used. For example, a "Relationship Manager" at one company may be called a "Global Account Executive" at a second company, and a "Major Account Representative" at a third company. Under your headline, you will want to include a qualifications section summarizing your strengths and accomplishments. It is not necessary to give this section a name, but you can title it SUMMARY if you prefer. To have impact, this summary should contain three to five sentences (not bullets) explaining the value that you can bring to the job and the organization. Ideally, it should use key words in the job description and reflect your research into the goals and challenges of the organization.

The goal here should be obvious; capture the attention of the reader so that the resume is almost immediately put into the short stack of resumes that will result in an initial job interview.

Do not use an OBJECTIVE instead of a SUMMARY on your resume unless you are a student or recent grad with little or no work history. If you need to use an OBJECTIVE, make it sound like a summary. For example:

OBJECTIVE

Obtain an internship where I can contribute and build upon my excellent knowledge of digital marketing, social media, and Advanced Excel, and utilize my interpersonal and problem solving skills.

An Objective is less appropriate for an experienced professional for the simple reason that an Objective speaks to what you want from the employer. **In a very competitive job market, the hiring manager or HR professional is primarily interested in what you can do for the organization.** Remember that you have only a few seconds to explain your value at the top of your resume.

In the summary statement in the sample resume below, note that sentence fragments are acceptable, while the word "I" does not appear.

Relevant

A resume is a marketing instrument, not a biography or legal document. It's critical to get across how you match up with the exact job requirements. Irrelevant information can also make it look like you are not fully in touch with the employer's hiring criteria. An effective resume clearly highlights only relevant positions, promotions, awards and accomplishments. This does not, however, mean that you should totally customize each resume. If this is necessary, you are probably not applying for the right job. The need for relevance is also a reason to keep your resume away from job boards and resume distribution services, and not hand them out indiscriminately at job fairs or networking events.

Measurable Accomplishments

Your experience bullets should reflect measurable accomplishments with action verbs. A good way to develop these is to use **CAR (Challenge, Action, and Result) stories**, which will be even more critical to develop for the interviewing process. When there was a job or organizational **Challenge**, what personal **Action** did you take to create a positive (preferably measurable) **Result**? Once you have the relevant accomplishments identified, you should list three to five of them in bullet form under each position. If you find it difficult to think of your accomplishments, try to remember back to times when you have been proud or excited by your work on a project and/or when you were praised by your coworkers or superiors.

These accomplishment bullets should replace statements containing only job duties, "Responsible for higher education marketing programs." Being responsible for something doesn't say anything about how well you did the job. Team efforts or results should not be included on your resume, "Assisted on strategic planning project," unless your own personal contribution to the effort is clear (you provided leadership or contributed a valuable new idea).

Your resume bullets should include action verbs. There are hundreds of possible action verbs that can be used in either present or past tense. For example, ones related to management skills may include: administer, analyze, assign, attain, achieve, build, chair, contract, consolidate, coordinate, delegate, deliver, direct, evaluate, execute, identify, negotiate, organize, plan, prioritize, produce, recommend, review, schedule, strengthen, supervise, and transform. Good action verbs for all positions include: created, increased, gained, reduced, improved, developed, saved, researched, transformed, and accomplished.

Results are usually related to increases in revenue, cost savings, process improvement (e.g., time, accuracy, and quality), and customer or employee satisfaction. If you did not have a direct impact on results, you can talk about how you made a valuable recommendation or provided significant support. Whenever possible, **quantify results with numbers,** and draw special attention to Profit & Loss management responsibility that you may have had.

- Increased (productivity by at least 15% at each of my last 3 employers)
- Improved (customer retention rates by 20%)
- Gained (30 new accounts valued at $1M)
- Saved (150,000 in rental costs)
- Reduced (employee turnover by 15% at my last company)
- Transformed (Steinfeld Hospital from being physician-centered to more patient-centered)

RESUME FORMAT: SEASONED PROFESSIONAL

JOE SAMPLE
jsample@email.com
555-555-5555
www.linkedin.com/in/joesample

EFFECTIVE RESUMES

HOTEL SALES MANAGEMENT PROFESSIONAL

Proactive business development team leader and individual contributor with strong sales skills developed in diverse hospitality environments. Progressive increases in responsibility due to exceptional interpersonal, relationship building, and negotiation skills. Exceptional success working with sports teams, associations, and Fortune 50 corporations.

KEY SKILLS (2 columns with four or five skills in each column)

Business and Channel Development	Customer Relationship Building
Sales Team Training	CRM forecasting and Market Analytics
Complex Negotiations	Process Reengineering

PROFESSIONAL EXPERIENCE

(3 to 5 accomplishment bullets under each company and position)

BROWNSTONE HOTEL, Chicago, IL
SALES DIRECTOR   2011-2014
Historic 75 room property located on the Gold Coast

- Personally booked 65% of all new sales revenues while growing existing account base by 25% in 2011

- Strengthened existing relationships with Steinfeld University programs resulting in 5% sales increase in 2012

- Successfully repositioned the hotel as upscale after major 2010 renovation

EDUCATION

(Leave off your graduation date if you are over 50. If you are a student or recent grad of any age, put this section with your expected or actual graduation date immediately below your Summary or Objective)

MBA, Operations and Marketing
Chicago Graduate School of Business
BS, Commerce and Marketing, University of North Dakota

If you have **CERTIFICATIONS, TRAINING** or **SPECIAL COURSEWORK, ADVANCED TECHNOLOGY SKILLS, PROFESSIONAL AFFILIATIONS, VOLUNTEER** or **COMMUNITY ACTIVITIES** and/or **ADDITIONAL ACTIVITIES**, add those at the end if relevant and space allows. If necessary to save space to stay on two pages, combine two categories (e.g., **CERTIFICATIONS & PROFESSIONAL AFFILIATIONS**).

Common Resume Questions

Q. What do you do if your last job was not relevant?
A. Do your best to make the first job listed on your resume relevant to the targeted position. This should be relatively easy if you have had a recent part-time, temporary, contract, or volunteer position that can be made relevant by highlighting transferable skills, strengths and knowledge.

There should be no attempt made to change your work history to make your resume more relevant. If you are tempted to do so, know that your complete work history can be retrieved online. It's very important to remember that **potential weaknesses within your resume, such as gaps in employment, can be neutralized if you can get to the hiring manager directly.** You can expect that the hiring manager will always be much more forgiving than his HR professional.

Q. Should I include non-work related activities?

A. Only include activities that can help reinforce a particular strength. For example, if leadership is important to the culture of the organization or the job, you might include a leadership position during your school years or military service. If discipline is important, you might list your marathon history or classical piano training. These can go under a section entitled **ADDITIONAL ACTIVITIES** or **LEADERSHIP ACTIVITIES** at the end of your resume.

Q. Does volunteer work belong on my resume?

A. Volunteer work should definitely be included on your resume, but it should be made as relevant to the position as possible. Include all your accomplishments as a volunteer under a heading called **VOLUNTEER ACTIVITIES** at the end of the resume unless you need the most recent one at the top of your resume to avoid showing a large gap since your last paid position. Please see the chapter titled *Volunteer Strategically* to better understand why volunteering during your job search is a great idea.

Q. Should I follow up after sending my resume?

A. Following up is critical, and shows that you care. If you are not following up, you may want to question if you are really interested in the job.

A few days after sending your resume and cover letter to the company, leave a less than 30 second voice **message before or after normal working hours** for the person to whom you sent your resume (remember that you will always be sending your resume to a specific person).

"Hello, Mr Jones. This is Steven Steinfeld. I sent my resume and cover letter in response to your posting for a rodeo marketing manager a few days ago, and want to make sure that you received them. I believe that I'm a strong candidate because of my education and experience, and my passion for the rodeo. I hope we can meet soon. When we do meet, I'd love to share some marketing ideas with you. I can be reached at 555-555-5555."

By leaving this message, you will bring attention to your resume and improve your chances to be called for a job interview. Before you leave the message, practice and time what you are going to say several times. Speak very slowly and clearly. If you cannot get out of your comfort zone to leave a voice mail, deliver a similar message through email although it may not be as effective.

If you send your resume and cover letter to HR, leave a simple message with the VP of HR or the HR specialist who works with applicants in your profession before or after normal working hours.

"Hello, Mrs Jones. This is Steven Steinfeld. I'm calling to make sure that you received my resume and cover letter in response to your posting for a rodeo marketing manager. I believe that I'm a strong candidate and am looking forward to the interview process. I can be reached at 555-555-5555."

Q. How do I identify the name, title and contact information of the hiring manager?

A. It's very important to remember that potential weaknesses within your resume, such as lack of experience, may be overlooked if you can get to the hiring manager directly.

All of the following are ways you can try to identify the hiring manager and his contact information. Think of yourself as a detective. Continue your detective work until you have everything you need.

- Informational interviews (see the chapter titled *The Power of the Informational Interview*).

- LinkedIn. Go to "Advanced People Search" and type in the name of the company and the title you would expect the hiring manager to hold. You can also ask other employees at the company within your LinkedIn network to point you to the hiring manager within the appropriate department for the particular job of interest (or directly provide you the email address for the hiring manager).

Once identified, send the hiring manager a LinkedIn invitation to connect (See the chapter titled *LinkedIn and Other Social Media* for an example of a message to include with your invitation). Join the maximum number of relevant LinkedIn Groups since you will have greater success receiving a positive response to your invitation to connect from a fellow group member. Once you are connected on LinkedIn, you will have access to his contact information.

- Google Advanced Search. Type in the name of the company and title you would expect the hiring manager to hold.

- Try subscription services such as Hoovers Database, Jigsaw.com or CareerShift.com. They may offer free trials.

- Search business publications such as chicagobusiness.com or the wsj.com for the names of executives and professionals in the news, on the move or recently promoted.

- Research the company's website for the names of senior management. If you send an executive an email, you might get a response asking you to send your resume to him directly, or he might give you the name and contact information for the appropriate hiring manager or HR professional. If he directs you to someone else, you can say that the senior manager asked you to contact him or submit your resume.

- Look at the website (and first level contacts at the company if you have any on LinkedIn) for clues on the email convention that the company uses. For example, if you see that other person's email address is steven_steinfeld@abccompany.com try addressing your email to someone else at his company to firstname_lastname@abccompany.com. If you send an email, make sure to include your LinkedIn address so that they can check out your profile.

> - Call the company. Try the receptionist or sales department. Say that you have some information to send him but do not have his email address. If asked, 'What information?" you can respond with "It's personal."

25 Additional Resume Tips

1. Use an uncomplicated Gmail address on your resume and for all of your job search correspondence. It sends a message of being current with technology. AOL, or a similarly out-of-fashion address, sends the opposite message (ignore this advice if you are applying for a job at AOL).

2. Put whatever name you normally use at the top of your resume. If you are normally known as Katie Brown, don't use Katherine J. Brown.

3. Your home address is optional, but you should include your LinkedIn address along with your email and cell phone information at the top of your resume if you have at least 100 contacts. Simplify your LinkedIn address under Settings at LinkedIn.com, and keep it professional.

4. If applying for a technical job, you might even consider including a QR code (vizibility.com) with a link to your social and professional profiles. If you have an online portfolio, you can include that link at the top as well. Use a template that is common to your industry and experiment with fonts including Times New Roman, Garamond and Arial.

EFFECTIVE RESUMES

5. Keep in mind that the emphasis today is on qualifications and achievements, not previous job titles or responsibilities.

6. If any of your previous companies are not well known, include a brief description of each company in slightly smaller font under the name of the company. You can easily get a one-line company description from its website.

7. Do not include skills taken for granted such as MS Office unless knowledge of the most recent MS Office software is important to the job; and avoid older technology references.

8. Only go back about 15 to 20 years on your experience. Anything older (and relevant), put in a category called **EARLY CAREER** with no dates, only company and job title.

9. If you are under 50, you should show your graduation dates. If you are over 50 you probably should not, unless you received a degree in the last 3 years. You are not fooling anyone when you omit your age, but you are avoiding highlighting your age if the reviewer is on the fence about the importance of restricting candidates to a certain age group.

10. Remove months, except the month of a recent or expected graduation date. Months not only get in the way of easy reading, they can also make a job that lasted only 13 months appear to have lasted up to two years. This is particularly important for the current year since even a job lasting a week can be seen to be much longer in duration if only the year is shown. Job duration will likely come up during the interview process, but **the purpose of your resume is only to get you the interview.** If you do show months, use the format: Feb 2014 instead of 2/14.

11. Tweak the narrative under your headline at the top of your resume to include at least a few key words used in a specific job description. Keep careful track of which version you sent to whom.

12. No matter what your age, if you have earned a degree within the last 3 years, put your education section near the top of your resume. Otherwise, your education section belongs near the bottom of your resume.

13. If you are currently studying for a degree or certification, show it in your Education section as expected (e.g., Expected May 2015).

14. Do not use pronouns in your Objective or Summary or when describing your accomplishments. For example, instead of saying "I developed," just say "Developed."

15. Do not include photos or personal information.

16. Do not include references or state that "references are available upon request," on your resume.

17. Do not underline, and avoid bolding except for headings.

18. Be consistent when with bullet point lists. Always end each bullet with a period, or always end each bullet without a period.

19. Do not include skills taken for granted such as MS Office unless knowledge of the most recent MS Office software is important to the job. Avoid non-relevant or older technology references.

EFFECTIVE RESUMES

20. If you have a paper resume and cover letter, both should be on good stock such as 24 lb. weight, white or off white linen paper.

21. Ask professionals in your field to review your resume in order to help you use language that is particularly relevant in your field.

22. If you have had your own one-person consulting firm, be sure to include specific client information, including your related accomplishments, under a category called "Representative Clients" in the PROFESSIONAL EXPERIENCE section.

23. Lock in your formatting by sending your resume as a .PDF or as a Word document in Restricted Editing/Read Only mode.

24. Beware of employing the over used expressions below, but don't be afraid to use any of these descriptors if necessary to highlight a key strength asked for in a job posting.

   a. Extensive experience
   b. Proven track record
   c. Motivated
   d. Dynamic
   e. Results-oriented
   f. Team player
   g. Entrepreneurial
   h. Innovative

> **25.** Read and reread your resume and then have two other people read it. You may get away with one typo or grammatical error, but not two. Resumes are considered an indication of your written communication ability and your attention to detail. It will also help if you print out your resume before you review it since you will see errors that you will not spot on a screen.

Don't worry about having your resume scanned by a computer through an applicant tracking system (ATS) used by large companies. Your goal should be to hand your resume to the hiring manager directly. Don't waste a lot of time filling in laborious online applications with the exception of those related to opportunities in government.

Compelling Cover Letters

> *"Excellence is to do a common thing in an uncommon way."*
>
> — Booker T. Washington

Even if a cover letter is not read (which is often the case), including one is expected and important since it shows that you are not broadcasting your resume to employers without putting in some effort. However, **I strongly suggest that you NOT include a cover letter if you can't write a good one or get someone with excellent writing skills to edit it for you.** Like your resume, your cover letter represents your ability to express yourself clearly, succinctly, and effectively. Of course, **if your resume is handed directly to the hiring manager, you won't need a cover letter.**

A good cover letter should be simple, easy and quick to read. Use no more than three or four short paragraphs, and customize each one.

The first paragraph should include how you heard of the job (e.g., job posting or referred by someone) and why you are interested, "I am responding to your rodeo marketing posting on Indeed.com. I am particularly interested in this position since I have been passionate about the rodeo since working for a major rodeo sponsor."

A really good cover letter includes a story, and can even be entertaining. In fact, if you are clever and feel that you need a way to differentiate yourself in your cover letter, make the first sentence an attention-grabber, "Why is a marketing professional from New York City interested in corralling a promotional rodeo job in Texas?" If you can do this well (bounce your grabber off a friend to make sure it's not too corny), your cover letter is likely to be fully read and remembered.

The second (and third paragraph if necessary) should state your potential value to the company. Start by aligning the 3 top reasons that you are a strong candidate with words and phrases from the job description in order of importance (the stuff you highlighted in GREEN).

Your cover letter should not be a rehash of your resume, but should either add something new to your resume, "My uncle was a rodeo cowboy, and because of my close relationship with him, I have a highly developed instinct for how the rodeo should be marketed," or highlight at least one important achievement within your resume that may be overlooked, "I worked at an advertising agency that managed a rodeo account at one of my past jobs, and contributed several innovative ideas to a very successful marketing campaign."

Mention something about your knowledge of the company that shows that you have done your research. One approach would be to align at least one company or hiring manager goal or challenge alongside your relevant experience and value. For example:

(Company Goal) "I read in your annual report that your company goal is to increase rodeo attendance by 5% per year."

(My Value) "I contributed innovative new ideas to a rodeo-related marketing communications program that increased event attendance by 10% in a single year. Based upon my research of your company, I believe that some of those ideas would be of value to your short term plans."

(Hiring Manager's Goal) "In your speech to the National Rodeo Association, you said, 'Developing creative social media marketing programs are becoming critical to your company's success.'

(My Value) "I recently received Certification in Social Media Marketing from Steinfeld University, and would love to discuss some of the new approaches that we studied with you."

Compare the following sample cover letter that follows the rules above to ones that you may have written or seen.

Hello Mr Steinfeld,

I am submitting this cover letter and my resume in response to the Account Coordinator position posted on Indeed.com. The position description not only sounds like it was written for me, but greatly appeals to my interest in joining a forward-thinking company that uses technology to enhance the customer experience.

I believe that I am a strong candidate for this position based on the following:

- I can bring a track record of success in account coordination to your company, with near perfect levels of client satisfaction.

- Throughout my career, I have been respected for my steadying influence in critical situations and my ability to break through bottlenecks to meet customer needs quickly without sacrificing quality.

- I have outstanding knowledge of the Customer Relationship Management (CRM) system that your company has just installed, and have developed a very effective training presentation that I can bring to your organization.

I look forward to meeting you in person to discuss both my qualifications and ideas on how to continue to improve account coordination and customer satisfaction at your company.

I will follow up with you in a few days to ensure that you received my resume and cover letter. I can be reached at 555-555-5555.

Thank you for your consideration.

Sincerely,

Lucy Cameron

Cover Letter Tips

- Put your cover letter into the body of your email rather than send it as an attachment.

- Do not sound too formal in your cover letters. Sound confident but friendly. An easy way to do this is to start the cover letter with "Hi" or "Hello."

- Do not attempt to use humor in your cover letter since it may be misunderstood.

- If you use more than two examples, use bullet points to add to the readability.

- Don't say that you are the "perfect candidate" or "the best candidate" since it may sound arrogant rather than confident, and you are not likely to be familiar with all of the other candidates.

- Do not attract attention to a competitive weakness, "Although I am not strong in tax preparation, my accounting skills are excellent."

- Whether or not it has been requested, if you have a strong portfolio, including work or presentation samples, consider including it as an attachment with your cover letter and resume (or provide a link to it on your resume or within your cover letter).

COMPELLING COVER LETTERS

- If you are applying for similar jobs, you can cut and paste some material from one cover letter to another, but customize every cover letter. If you do cut and paste, be sure to proofread the new letter very carefully.

- Remember that your goal is to send your resume and cover letter directly to the hiring manager. If you do wind up sending it to HR, put in the time to get the name of a real person rather than addressing your letter to "Hiring Manager," "Dear Sir," or "To Whom It May Concern." That extra personalization will get your resume and cover letter much more attention.

Strategic Networking

*"I hear and I forget. I see and I remember.
I do and I understand."*

– Confucius

You may have been told hundreds of times that you should network during your job search, but you may not know why it is critically important, or how to effectively go about networking with other professionals. This chapter will help you overcome your concerns and teach you how to network step by step, even if you are shy or introverted.

Job search networking is not about asking for job leads, and it's not about approaching everyone in the same way. Your top networking goal should be to connect with as many people as possible who can give you the information, advice, referrals and recommendations you need to effectively connect with hiring managers and the people who influence them.

Consider that you have less than a 5% chance of an interview if you submit your resume to HR without a recommendation — about a 50% chance if your resume is personally introduced into the HR department by an employee — and close to 100% if you are recommended to the hiring manager by a trusted friend or colleague of that manager.

Now imagine that you and I are both interviewing for a job. We are both qualified, but you are almost certain to be seen as the better candidate. A friend or colleague of the hiring manager mentions to him, "I understand that you will be interviewing Steven Steinfeld tomorrow. I'm not sure if he interviews well, but I'm sure that he would be a great addition to your marketing department. He's passionate about the rodeo, has great problem solving skills, and comes up with really creative promotional ideas. If I were you, I would grab him before a competitor does. The guy is awesome!" Which of us do you think is going to get the job?

Your goal should be to get to the hiring manager before there is a job posting, and preferably before anyone knows that there is going to be a job opening. The only way to accomplish this is through strategic networking.

Job search coaches used to say that about 60% of jobs landed were the direct or indirect result of networking. Today, we say **that landing a professional job is related to networking up to 90% of the time**. Even so, very few job seekers spend 90% of their time networking. In fact, they often spend relatively little time. This is because the idea of networking can appear daunting, mostly because it will require that you get out of your comfort zone.

STRATEGIC NETWORKING

On average, 45% of all employees hired in the U.S. are referred to the company by a current employee, and some companies hire up to 80% of their new employees on the basis of an employee recommendation. In addition to current employees, interview candidates are often referred by former employees and trusted and influential allies (friends, colleagues, former colleagues) of hiring managers.

Even if an employee or ally of the hiring manager is not directly familiar with your work, you have a good chance of being referred for a job interview if you can impress him with your value statement and personality in a networking interaction or at an informational interview. If that same employee or advisor can speak glowingly about your value from personal experience, you have an almost 100% chance of being hired if you do well on your interview.

Networking allows you to bypass the gatekeepers in HR who are there to block your direct contact with the managers who make hiring decisions. Unless your skill set and experience is an almost perfect match to the listed job qualifications, your resume will be quickly dismissed by HR unless it has been brought to them by an employee. Even if you are an almost perfect match, your resume may never get read by a live person in a large company, and may go unread at the bottom of a 500 resume pile in a small to medium sized company. **Whether or not you submit your resume through HR, you should assume that you will not be called for an interview without direct contact with a hiring manager, a personal contact of the hiring manager, or an employee.**

In addition to helping you land your next job, and perhaps positioning you for another one down the road, networking provides personal and community relationships that can be extremely important to your sense of well-being during your job search. Start networking by getting the word out to everyone within your inner circle— and to alumni, former colleagues, and other allies who you feel will be especially supportive.

The Elements of Effective Networking

Balance Quality and Quantity

Whether you network on-line or in-person, there is almost no such thing as a bad network contact, since even the most unlikely person may be able to help move you closer to your goals.

Effective networking requires relationship building, and that requires time and effort. Of all of the contacts you make, it's advised that you concentrate on building relationships with a relatively small number of people who have extensive networks (often with 500+ LinkedIn contacts) and who indicate a genuine interest in building a reciprocal relationship with you.

Strategy, Planning, and Goals

One of your job search goals should be building your contact base by a specific number each week. When you go to a networking event (set up Google Alerts and check www.meetup.com for local events in your industry), you should go with a plan. Your plan should include initiating conversations, tailoring your value statement to each person you meet, and spending between three to five minutes speaking to each individual. This will turn out much better than running around collecting business cards.

If you are an introvert, an example of an effective strategy at a networking event would be to wait for people to leave a group or approach people who are standing alone in order to be able to engage one-on-one. Another strategy would be to bring along your extroverted friend John so that he can bring you into a conversation that may prove valuable:

John (speaking to Joe, a corporate Marketing VP): "Joe, Have you met my friend Steven Steinfeld? He's an amazing marketing guy who's been investigating joining a company in your industry."

STRATEGIC NETWORKING

Joe: "Really? Steven, your timing may be great. I'm planning to hire a marketing professional to handle our new rodeo account. Please send me your resume."

Steven: "Joe, why don't we get together next week? I can bring my resume along and answer any questions you may have. As it turns out, rodeo marketing is one of my specialties, and I may be able to share some ideas that may be of immediate interest to your company when we meet."

Joe: "Great idea! Here's my business card with my company's address. Why don't we meet at my office at 3 pm on Tuesday or Wednesday?"

Steven: "Tuesday is perfect! Here's my business card. I'll see you at 3 pm on Tuesday."

Steven now leaves as quickly as possible before Joe asks a question that might disqualify him before he gets to their meeting.

Before the meeting, Steven spends time meeting researching Joe's company and successful rodeo industry marketing programs, tweaks his resume, researches Joe on LinkedIn and through a Google Advanced Search, and looks for mutual contacts who may be able to influence Joe directly or indirectly before or after their meeting. Steven sends Joe a meeting confirmation email on Monday with his cell phone number in case Joe needs to change the day or time of the meeting.

> Subj: Meeting Confirmation
>
> Joe, I am confirming the meeting that we arranged for tomorrow at 3pm. I am very much looking forward to discussing the rodeo marketing position with you. In case there is a need for a change in schedule, please contact me on my cell phone at 555-555-5555.
>
> Thank you.
>
> Steven Steinfeld

Effective networking takes some planning and organization. Start your job search networking plan by mapping your contacts as shown below:

Start Mapping and Prioritizing Your Network	
Friends, Relatives, Neighbors and Spouse/Partner's Network	Current or Former Classmates, Faculty and Alumni
Current or Former Co-workers or Managers	Family Business Connections (Accountant, Attorney, Banker, Insurance Agent)
Volunteer, Community, Religious, Political and Sports Groups or Clubs	Professional Associations or Organizations

- Connecting with people in your inner circle is a good way to "warm up" before talking to people with who you may be less comfortable.
- Prioritize contacts according to their ability to hire you, connect you with hiring managers and employees at target companies, give you company or industry information, provide valuable career advice or guidance, evaluate your value statement, and/or advocate effectively for you.
- When you connect with these contacts:
  - Give them your value statement
  - Ask them what they know about organizations on your target list
  - Ask for informational interview contacts
  - Ask only for information and/or advice
  - Look for some way to repay them for helping you

STRATEGIC NETWORKING

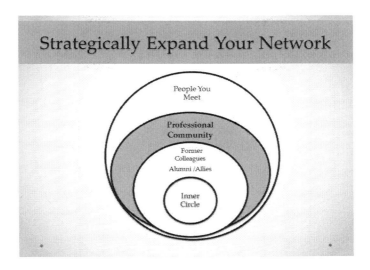

Base Your Networking on GIVING

When you attend a networking event, go as a problem solver. For example, recommend books and articles, offer connections with people in your network, spread news of upcoming conferences or meetings, or suggest resources that may have been overlooked. Because you will be perceived as being concerned and helpful, they will start to ask you questions in order to determine how best to return the favor, and will listen very carefully to your value statement. Use this same approach with everyone you connect with on LinkedIn and in your daily life.

Engage as Many People as You Can

Get in the habit of finding a pretext to start a conversation. If you are an introvert, set a goal to interact with at least one stranger every day. It will help you get out of your comfort zone. For example, the following would be a conversation that you might have while sitting next to someone on the bus:

You: "Excuse me. Is that the new iPhone?"

New Contact: "Yes"

You: "How do you like it?"

New Contact: "My company just bought it for me. So far, I love it."

You: "What kind of work do you do?"

New Contact: "I'm the Vice-President of a consumer products company. What do you do?"

You: (Giving a short version of your value statement) "I'm a social worker currently looking for a new opportunity to utilize my case management and Spanish language skills.

New Contact: "It's a small world. My wife is a social worker at Steinfeld Hospital."

You: "Would it be asking too much for you to introduce me to her? I could really use some information and advice, and it would only take about 20 minutes."

New Contact: "She's pretty busy but I think she'll agree to meet you. Here's my card. Send me your resume and I'll arrange it. By the way, I'm Tom Smith."

You: "I can't thank you enough Tom. I'm Liza de Quito. I'll be sure to send you my resume today."

Think I'm simplifying the ease of getting an informational interview that might even lead to a job offer? **You'll never know if you don't try**!

Understand the Networking Ladder

Think of networking effectiveness as a ladder. On the bottom rung are contacts that cannot help you because they do not know what you want or for which job you're best suited. This is because you say something vague such as "I'm open to anything," or are not specific when talking about the job you are seeking, "I'm looking for an international job," or cannot explain your value clearly, or are too embarrassed to ask for help, "I was laid off from my job but I'm taking a break before looking for new opportunities."

One rung up on the ladder, you'll find people who are unlikely to help because you are not connecting with them or they see you lack confidence, "Steven, I am an accountant, but am a little rusty since I have been out of work for over a year. Can you help me connect me with some accounting firms that might be willing to hire me anyway?"

Another rung up are the nice people who will agree to help if asked, but they may not put much time and effort into it, "Sure Steven, send me a copy of your resume. I'll ask around and let you know if I hear of anything."

On the top rungs of the ladder are contacts that will genuinely offer to help and will follow-through on their promises, sometimes even actively talking about you to hiring managers without being asked. However, **people will only help you if you have a good value statement and deliver it with confidence.**

Follow-Through with Gratitude and Reciprocation

It's critical that you follow-through with gratitude and reciprocation after a networking encounter. If someone does something for you, ask if there is something specific that you can do for him now or in the near future. If at an event, get a business card and write down the follow-up that you promised her on the back. It's more important for you to get a business card than to give out your own, but you should also have a professional business card to help others follow-up with you (www.vistaprint.com or a local printer).

Build Networking Equity

Continue to update your best contacts. This can be in the form of an email about every six weeks with a piece of information that may be of interest or value to each of them:

> Subj: Thank You
> Dan,
> Thanks again for helping me connect with Don Jones. I wanted to let you know that I am still interviewing for marketing positions, but have expanded my search to the pharmaceutical industry. I you know of anyone who might be able to give me some current industry information or advice, please let me know. In any event, I am attaching an article from the Wall Street Journal that I think would be of interest to you.
> Best Regards,
> Steven

During your job search, end with an update on how your search is going and thank them for the support that they have given to you along the way.

Consider Developing a Handbill

A handbill is a one-page condensed version of your resume that summarizes your strengths and experiences, and also lets a networking contact know which specific industries, organizations and jobs you are targeting. A handbill is expected at certain networking events for senior level executives, but it is also useful to send to someone who sincerely wants to help you arrange informational interviews. You will be amazed how many people you know or meet will know someone at one of your targeted companies (or a similar company).

The format of your handbill should be in a similar format to your resume but should only include the following:

- Your name, contact information, and LinkedIn address
- Profile (one paragraph)
- Key Accomplishments (3-5 bullet points)
- List of Top Strengths (3-5)

STRATEGIC NETWORKING

- Professional Experience (last 3-5 employers with Job Title – no dates)
- Targeted Industries (up to 5)
- Targeted Positions (up to 5)
- Targeted companies (up to 15)

SAMPLE HANDBILL
JOE SAMPLE
555-555-5555
jsample@gmail.com
www.linkedin.com/in/joesample

PROFILE

KEY ACCOMPLISHMENTS

KEY STRENGTHS	PROFESSIONAL EXPERIENCE
TARGET POSITIONS	TARGET INDUSTRIES
TARGET COMPANIES	TARGET COMPANIES

10 Tips for In-Person Networking Activity

1. Be open, friendly and genuine. You should always feel that you are talking to a friend.

2. Give everyone you meet a big SMILE and firm handshake while making direct eye contact. Shake hands for six seconds since research tells us that it takes that long for a handshake to establish a good connection.

3. Keep your value statement and your background story short. If what you say is compelling; others will almost certainly ask you to elaborate.

4. Listen carefully to what the other person is saying, and ask for clarification until you understand how you can be of help to him. Look for things you have in common with the people you meet, "You love the rodeo? Hey, I love the rodeo!"

5. If you don't know something, admit it. People will appreciate your honesty, it will build credibility, and you will learn something new.

6. Always look presentable during your job search. You never know who you might meet when you leave the house.

7. When introduced to someone at an event, repeat his name a couple of times to remember it. Instead of saying, "How did you hear about this event," say "Joe, how did you hear about this event,"

8. If you know that certain people are going to a networking event, check their profiles on LinkedIn to get some information that may be helpful in starting conversations.

9. Always be reading at least one recently published book. You can use it to make conversation during networking events, "Have you read 3 Steps to Your Best Job Ever? I think you would find it helpful." You can also use it as an excuse to connect with the other person after the event, 'If you give me your business card, I will email you a link to the book that I just mentioned, and I will send you an invitation to connect on LinkedIn."

10. Take advantage of networking opportunities, including those provided by professional organizations, social networking, and your alma mater. Concentrate on ones where you might meet people who are currently employed in your industry.

LinkedIn and Other Social Media

"Social media allows me to pick my times for social interaction."

-Guy Kawasaki, Silicon Valley Entrepreneur

Did you know that more than 80% of employers will post jobs and check profiles on social media—mostly on LinkedIn — and up to 3M job seekers per month credit social media with helping their job searches?

I have included information in this chapter that can be of value to job hunting professionals who wish to maximize the use of LinkedIn and other social media. **Much of this information, apart from information related to LinkedIn, is optional.** On the other hand, **every job hunter should be familiar enough with popular social media services such as Facebook, Twitter and Pinterest to understand why and how they are being used, and understand that LinkedIn is your best and most necessary job search resource.**

LinkedIn is a worldwide electronic networking tool created specifically for professionals to help in researching people and companies, industry trends, and relevant business topics. **The more active you are on LinkedIn, the better you can tell your story, establish your credibility, develop your reputation, and make valuable connections.**

10 Reasons to Use LinkedIn

1. As a door opener to face-to-face networking with people who can give you informational and job interviews

2. Identify target companies

3. Identify new job opportunities

4. Prepare for interviews by researching employers and interviewers

5. Request introductions that can reinforce your value and enhance your credibility

6. Connect with former co-workers and classmates

7. Find and exchange information with professionals in your field

8. Demonstrate your networking and social media skills

9. Create a global presence online. In most cases, your LinkedIn profile will be near or at the top of a Google search of your name

10. Enhance your visibility and marketability so that HR and 3rd party recruiters can find and research you online For example, many companies search candidates' LinkedIn and other social-media accounts to get a better feel for a candidate's personality and to judge how well he communicates.

If you are new to LinkedIn, know that getting started is easy, and there are many LinkedIn tutorials, including videos, online (Google search "LinkedIn tutorials") in addition to the instructions given on LinkedIn. Once you are comfortable with the basics, add my favorite tips below to enhance your LinkedIn experience and improve your results.

LINKEDIN AND OTHER SOCIAL MEDIA

My Top 15 LinkedIn Tips for Job Seekers

It is best to follow along on LinkedIn as you read the following tips. Please note that while LinkedIn features sometimes change or are added or deleted, your objectives should remain the same.

1. Match Your Profile to Your Resume

    Your resume should speak to your target audience. Since you should not have multiple profiles on LinkedIn (and a good reason not to be sending out 10 completely different resumes), your profile should match the most preferred and realistic opportunity you are targeting. **Make sure to add a professional looking photo.** Most employers will check your LinkedIn profile before offering you an interview, and the first thing they will look for is a professional photo. Your photo is also required to complete your profile to the 100% level. 100% completion makes you 40X easier to find by recruiters who are scanning LinkedIn continuously for job candidates.

2. Have a Strong Headline and Summary

    Let's say your last title was "Sales & Marketing Professional." Many people naturally leave that as their headline; but it's too broad and says nothing about what they actually do. Use a headline statement that really describes your expertise and talent, such as, "**Hospitality Sales and Marketing Director - Expertise in Education and Association Sectors.**" Then further develop it by creating a summary about your career that describes your passion for your work and your past successes. LinkedIn also gives you the option to add media samples to your profile.

3. **Customize Your Invitations**

   It is common and acceptable to send an invitation to connect to a professional you do not know without an introduction—but do not send the standard invitation, "I would like to add you to my LinkedIn network." Send a personal LinkedIn message mentioning something or someone you have in common, and don't hesitate to appeal to his ego. For example, you might send the following invitation:

   > Joe, I am expanding my LinkedIn network to include respected marketing professionals who graduated from our alma mater, Steinfeld University. I am very happy to share my network with you. Please let me know if I can be of assistance personally or professionally.

   In order to get this personalization option, you must click on the "Connect" link on the person's actual profile. Avoid sending a broadcast invitation to multiple people since you won't be able to personalize each one.

   Start with people in your inner circle plus your current and former classmates and co-workers, and expand from there. Before sending the invitation, read through each person's profile. You may pick up hints on specific ways you can offer to assist them immediately that you can include in your message. If you don't know them very well, you may want to remind them who you are, who you have in common, and let them know why you think it might be mutually beneficial to connect with them. **Don't mention your job search within your invitations**, but once you are connected, use their email addresses to ask them for informational interviews and/or introductions to others who can provide you with information and/or advice.

   Don't worry if people don't respond immediately. Some will respond quickly and some slowly, and some may never respond; but that's

LINKEDIN AND OTHER SOCIAL MEDIA

one of the things that will help you determine your most promising LinkedIn relationships.

Avoid getting rejected or restricted. Make sure your LinkedIn profile is complete and up-to-date. When you request to connect with someone, he will review your profile before responding. If your profile isn't optimized and professional, it will increase your chances of getting rejected. Also, always give a reason to connect. If you are rejected or ignored by too many LinkedIn contacts, you will be blocked from further invitations without knowing the person's email address. When you personalize your connection request, be honest if you are not connected in any way:

> Joe, We haven't met, but I came across your profile and share your interest in (insert something specific you learned from their profile or Google Advanced Search on his name). I'm happy to share my network with you, and I'd love to learn more about your work (industry or company).

Consider inviting me to join your network (www.linkedin.com/in/stevensteinfeld) to increase your number of second level contacts. I have a large number of LinkedIn contacts, and my profile is in the top 1% of all LinkedIn profiles viewed. I will accept your invitation if you mention that you are a reader of this book, and you will have many more 2nd level contacts.

4. **Bring Your Profile to the Top of Search Results**

   Since recruiters are constantly searching LinkedIn for candidates using keywords and job titles, you will want your profile to appear as high as possible in the results of those searches.

After you have completed your profile to the 100% level, go to "Advanced People Search."

Enter keywords that describe your targeted position.

Enter your location.

Hit "Search." Does your profile appear on one of the first few pages of results?

Now open the profile of the person that appeared at top of the first page of the search results. The keywords that LinkedIn used to filter the search will be highlighted.

Repeat the search using job titles instead of keywords.

Now go to your own profile and increase the use of the most important keywords and job titles that you believe recruiters at your targeted jobs would most likely use when scanning LinkedIn for candidates. Note that the more specific you make your keywords and job titles, and the more times they appear, the higher your position will be in a LinkedIn search.

5. **Identify Target Companies**

   Put keywords and/or industries into the search box under Companies (e.g., financial analyst manufacturing). Filter the results by geography. Add companies of interest to your targeted company list, and follow them for information, insights and new job announcements.

6. **Get LinkedIn Recommendations**

   It is helpful to get from six to ten strong recommendations from your former managers, clients or colleagues to highlight your strengths and show that you were a valued associate. Make sure that you give your recommenders ideas on what attributes they might include in your recommendation, but don't write it for them unless they specifically ask you to do so. You can also collect Endorsements under Skills & Expertise, but I don't recommend this unless you can get an impressive number of contacts to endorse your most important and relevant skills. Generally, the more Recommendations and Endorsements you give, the more you will receive, but you should not give an insincere Recommendation or Endorsement just to get one in return.

7. **Understand Where People with Your Background are Coming From and Going Next**

    Use LinkedIn Company Home pages or "Advanced People Search" to find network contacts working at your target companies. The Company page will also show you the top skill sets of the employees who work there and the top companies from which they came.

    Also use "Advanced People Search" to find people who worked at your target companies in the past and where they have gone after leaving the company. You can use this information to help broaden your list of prospective employers within a specific industry, and you may be able to find some informational interview contacts who can give you honest feedback about companies on your target list.

    Look especially for people who have recently joined the company. You might contact them asking for an informational interview, "I have been researching your company and noticed that you recently joined. Can we spend a few minutes together in person or on the phone so that I can understand why you joined the company?" If you get the interview, ask the contact how he got the job. If that fails, you can still examine his background to try to understand what made him attractive to his new employer.

8. **Add 3rd Party Recruiters**

   If you want to add "outside the company" recruiters to your network, concentrate on recruiters who specialize in your industry.

9. **Benefit from Joining LinkedIn Groups**

   Participating in groups on a regular basis is a relatively easy way to make new contacts and build credibility in your profession. It is also an easy way to come across articles and videos that may be of interest to people in your network.

   If you don't know what group to join, click on "Groups You May Like" to get started. Join up to 50 groups and contribute to two or three group discussions on a regular basis (try to add a unique point of view). Over time, you will learn which groups are the most valuable to you, and you can exchange the less valuable ones for new ones. If you are getting too much group email, adjust your settings to get updates once per week or filter them to go into an email folder.

10. **Customize Your URL**

    Click on "Settings" (under your name) and go to "Helpful Links" on the next page. Click on "Edit Your Public Profile," and simplify your LinkedIn domain name under "Customize My URL." Once customized, add it to the top of your resume and the bottom of your emails.

11. **Use the LinkedIn Job Board**

    When you access a job within the "Jobs" tab, LinkedIn will immediately show the contacts in your network that can connect you to the company. You can also save the searches that give you the best results, and set them up to alert you to new job postings by email.

12. Update Your Profile or Status Multiple Times per Week

The more active you are on LinkedIn, the more your profile will be visible to recruiters. To be more visible, add or modify a skill or put something of interest (job fair or networking event you are attending) into a status update one or more times per week to let your network know that you are still actively engaged in job search.

13. Join Your Alumni Group

Go to LinkedIn.com/college and your alumni network. At the bottom of the page, you will have an opportunity to join your LinkedIn Alumni group.

14. Pay Attention to "People You May Know"

You might be amazed how many excellent contacts LinkedIn will find for you.
Check this often and thoroughly. It will also give you an easy, casual way to contact the other person, "LinkedIn may be smarter than we are. It suggested we connect...."
Also look carefully at other suggestions that LinkedIn makes concerning jobs, groups, and industry or company information that may be of interest to you.

15. Check Experimental Features

Occasionally, you may want to check for new LinkedIn experimental features that may be of value to you at http://engineering.linkedin.com

Social Media Tips

- Start by doing a Google search on yourself to see what comes up. For one thing, you will see what potential employers may see. If there is something you do not want an employer to see, you will not be able to delete it unless you contact the webmaster of the specific page. If you are able to get more recent and positive listings, they will push less positive listings lower down in a Google search.

- If you are active on social networking sites such as Facebook or Google+, I suggest that you keep these non-business sites separate and **restrict access to only your close circle of friends**. Employers may check your Facebook account to get an idea of your character. Even if you have nothing to hide, some postings may reflect poorly on you. If you are concerned about things that might embarrass you if seen by a prospective employer, go through your timeline and "unlike" or "delete" those posts.

- To be safe, closely monitor your pages and remove all posts that may be controversial. If you still insist on using them for work related networking, establish separate accounts or circles.

- Always keep a positive attitude and ensure proper English grammar on LinkedIn and your other social networking sites.

- Use the same professional LinkedIn photo, and the exact same name, for all of your social networking sites, including Facebook.

LINKEDIN AND OTHER SOCIAL MEDIA

- Utilize Twitter to create opportunities for informational interviews by interacting with people connected to your target industry. It is also a good way to stay tuned in to what' target companies, some of which tweet new job postings. Start with a professional-sounding bio under 140-characters since the rest of a longer bio will not be immediately visible. Go to hashtags.org to find Twitter feeds that may be helpful (e.g., #jobhunter, #boomer), and to find out when they are most active.

- Post diverse content to drive traffic to your social media sites such as questions, insights, recommendations, and links to articles of interest, videos or books.

- If you have an impressive work portfolio, you can put it on LinkedIn, Squidoo.com, a personal website, pinterest.com and/or one of the online platforms available for that express purpose. Also use Pinterest.com to understand the culture of some of your target organizations, and for career and job search information. Consider creating a portfolio on Pinterest to highlight your work and creativity. Pinterest can also give you some insight into interests that might be helpful during the Discovery step — not to mention giving you a fun diversion from your job searching.

- If you are pursuing a job where social media or networking activity or expertise is important, an employer may ask you for your score. Get to understand Klout and check your Klout score at Klout.com.

- If you're a particularly good writer, place comments on respected blogs in your field. Not sure which ones? Check out alltop.com or post as a guest blogger on EzineArticles.com.

- As tempting as it might be, don't get into an argument or criticize someone else's opinion in a LinkedIn or Twitter posting.

- Utilize Twitter (and the Twellow search directory) effectively by interacting with people in your target industry, creating opportunities for telephone and in-person meetings. If you want to show your comfort with Twitter, consider one of the many Twitter apps that will help you quickly build a following. Some are free and some require purchase (e.g. Tweet Adder).

The Power of the Informational Interview

"There is nothing men are so generous of as advice."
— Francois de La Rochefoucauld, 17th Century French Author

An informational interview is a meeting in which a job seeker asks for first-hand career, industry and company information and/or advice rather than ask about job leads or job openings. Informational interviews have made the difference for many of my clients, and it's where you want your networking to take you. **Scheduling and holding in-person informational interviews should be at or near the top of your weekly goals.**

Since you never know where an informational interview may lead, the perfect informational interviewee is someone who can offer you a job. The second best is someone who is close enough to the hiring manager to introduce you or hand-carry your resume to her. However, most often the person who gives you the informational interview is what we call a company "insider." This person can be anyone in the company who can provide you with the information that you need, and can get you closer to the hiring manager if the company is of interest to you. If you concentrate on a specific company, you may eventually get to the hiring manager through a series of informational interviews.

Sometimes an informational interview will lead directly to a job offer with little or no competition, but this should not be your expectation or your only reason to pursue these interviews. There are many other important benefits to holding these interviews during both the Discovery and Action steps of your job search.

Informational Interview Benefits (Discovery Step)

- Understand the ideal skills, strengths, knowledge, education, experience, and credentials or certifications required for specific jobs. The answers will help you validate if a company, job or industry that you are targeting is a great fit.

- Expand your job market and industry information. What are the current challenges and goals within the industry? How does that align with what you offer? In the course of the interview, you may also come to know that there is an excellent job market for your targeted position, or you might find out just the opposite.

- Discover relevant job titles. Often the same job has different titles at different companies. Learning as many of these job titles as possible will help you expand your use of key words in online searches, and may help guide your choice of what to use as your resume and LinkedIn headlines.

- Find out about jobs and career paths you have not considered or didn't know existed. ("Steven, I know that you are looking at sales positions, but have you looked into becoming a fund raiser? I think you would be great and you would have a chance to get a job at my organization.")

- Practice your value statement and C.A.R. (Challenge, Action, and Result) stories (see the chapter titled *Mastering Job Interviews* for a full explanation of C.A.R.), and talk candidly about your career goals to test the reaction.

- Test the reaction to the reasons behind your last one, two, or three job moves. See if your explanations elicit questions that can help you improve your answers in the future.

- Get resume advice from someone in your field with a successful resume. Ask that same person to share his own resume. No one can provide the same insight to your resume as someone who is successfully engaged in your target job.

Informational Interview Benefits (Action Step)

- Gain first-hand information about company goals, challenges, and immediate needs. This will help you tailor your resume and formulate your questions and answers for a potential job interview. You may also find that there is a company reorganization or expansion coming soon, or that employees in your targeted job are leaving for good reasons. Such information can be of value to you in deciding if and when to pursue a job interview.

- Meet potential recommenders and hiring managers. The person sitting across from you on an informational interview may be your next boss or the influential colleague who can introduce you with a recommendation to the hiring manager.

- Understand the culture of the organization. The informational interview is a great way to identify a potential mismatch before you spend more time pursuing a job at that company with an unacceptable culture.

- Build confidence for job interviews. The more positive feedback, and the more you practice interviewing, the more your confidence will grow.

- Understand if you are connecting. You will quickly grow to understand when you are not connecting. If you are not connecting, you will know that you need to make adjustments in your communication style, answers, value statement, and/or your appearance. You will know you are not connecting if there is no offer of follow-up help.

- Expand your network by asking for referrals to at least two other professionals at the end of each informational interview.

Q. Who should I target for an informational interview?

A. The best informational interview candidate is the hiring manager himself. The second best is someone who is close enough to the hiring manager to introduce you or hand-carry your resume to him or HR, preferably with a strong recommendation. Sometimes the person who gives you the informational interview will only give you information and advice, but if you can get a referral from him to another employee, you will eventually get your resume to the hiring manager or HR. Start by focusing on anyone with who you have something in common. Be sure to include some informational interviews with professionals with a similar background who have been recently hired in your same field to understand how they overcame their job search challenges.

Q. How do I handle the informational interview?

A. Always keep in mind that an informational interview should be handled in the same professional way you handle a job interview, but

THE POWER OF THE INFORMATIONAL INTERVIEW

should be treated more as a conversation than a question and answer session.

Spend the first few minutes of the interview asking the interviewee about his own experience with the company (e.g., how he was hired, his career prior to coming to company, outside interests, family). People love to talk about themselves. In fact, the more you allow people to talk, the more they will think that it was a wonderful conversation. Mention or comment on anything that comes up that you have in common in order to strengthen your connection and improve your chances for being helped.

Continue by briefly explaining: how you got interested in his field, your education and most relevant strengths and skills, any work or volunteer experience you have already had in the field, and the steps you have taken to learn more, including the people in the field you have already met and the advice they have given you.

Then **ask up to five carefully selected open-ended questions in priority order** since you may never get to the last one if the other person's answers are long or he asks you lots of questions. Select questions from the list below to ask, noting the similarities and differences between the questions in the Discovery and Action steps. For example, in the Discovery step, you will want to ask questions about his field and industry, but in the Action step, you will want to ask questions about his specific company. If there are questions not listed here that you really need or want answered, be sure to include them. **Always make time to include a question at the end that asks the interviewee for additional people you should interview.**

Sample Questions to Ask During an Informational Interview (Discovery Step)

- If you were starting out today, would you choose the same path for yourself?
- What do you find most satisfying about your job and field?
- What kind of challenges does your work provide?
- What are the important new trends in your field?
- What do you see as the main criteria for success in your field?
- Based upon what I have told you about myself, what jobs do you think I am best qualified for in your industry?
- What's the best advice you can give me?
- Would you be willing to review and critique my resume?
- Who do you suggest I talk with next? May I use your name? (always try for at least two or three referrals)

THE POWER OF THE INFORMATIONAL INTERVIEW

Sample Questions to Ask During an Informational Interview (Action Step)

- What encouraged you to join your company?

- What qualifications does your company look for in the job I am targeting?

- What do you see as the main criteria for success at your company in the position I am targeting (skills, strengths, knowledge, education or certifications, experience)?

- What are your companies short and long term challenges? Are these typical for your industry?

- What sort of people do well in the company and in the position that I am targeting?

- What else is important to know about the company?

- Can you tell me about the person who manages the department where I would work if I decide to pursue a job at the company?

- Who do you suggest I talk with next? May I use your name? (always try for at least two or three referrals)

- Is there any final advice you would like to offer?

Q. How is an informational interview different from a job interview?
A. If you are contacting a prospective hiring manager, there is very little difference between contacting him for an informational interview or a

job interview. They should generally be treated the same way. The only difference is that calling for an informational interview puts less stress on the hiring manager since you are only asking for information and advice. An informational interview also opens the door to the hidden job market (job opportunities that are not posted).

Q. Doesn't the person you are contacting for an informational interview assume that you want him to help you land a job?
A. Keep in mind that a job that is the wrong fit will not be sustainable, and that your main goal should be to ask questions that will allow you to determine your fit for the job, company, or industry. If the other person senses that you are sincerely interested in getting helpful career information and advice, he will be less likely to question your motives. Your sincerity should come across when you ask for an informational interview and at the interview itself.

Q. Should I conduct myself differently than I would on a job interview?
A. No. The same basics apply. For example: be on time, make a compelling value statement, demonstrate strong interpersonal skills, and show him that you have researched his industry and company.

Q. What should I avoid saying?
A. Few people you plan to approach for job search help, including on an informational interview, will be interested in hearing about your personal wants or needs. "I need to find a job soon to make my car payment."
Your conversation should include your value statement, but do not take the time to give lots of details about your past job history, personal strengths,

or accomplishments. Also, you should not ask him questions about current job openings unless he brings up the subject.

The Informational Interview Process

1- **Ask for the interview**

Send an email or LinkedIn message with your reason for meeting and a suggested meeting place. You can use a standard format, but you should tailor your message for each situation.

In your message:
- Introduce yourself and mention how you got his name (e.g., referral, came across his LinkedIn profile while researching his industry, company or position). If possible, point out something you have in common.
- Explain your reason for the request. **Only ask for information or advice.** If asking about a job opening is the focus of your call or email, and there are no posted openings that fit your background, the person has a valid reason not to meet with you.
- Suggest a 20 minute meeting at a coffee shop near his office since he will be less likely to be distracted, and more likely to engage in casual conversation, outside of his office. However, if he would rather meet at his office or somewhere away from his office, agree without objection.

Sample Email Requests

Subj: Meeting Request

Hi Dick,

We haven't met, but I came across your profile on the Steinfeld Business School alumni page on LinkedIn. I am a fellow alumnus who is looking for a new marketing opportunity in New York City.

It would be a great help if you would be kind enough to meet with me for 20 minutes over coffee near your office within the next two weeks to help me answer a few questions about the advertising industry job market in NYC, and offer me some advice. Please let me know where and when it would be most convenient to meet.

Thank you for considering my request. I am very much looking forward to meeting you.

Sincerely,

Lucy Cameron

Subj: Referral from Steven Steinfeld

Hi John,

A mutual friend, Steven Steinfeld, suggested that I contact you. I recently told him that I am potentially interested in investigating opportunities at your company. I have researched the company and was impressed by what I read, especially the innovative new social media strategy that is being deployed.

Before deciding how to proceed, it would be very helpful if you would be kind enough to provide me with some insights into the company.

THE POWER OF THE INFORMATIONAL INTERVIEW

> For example, I would like to talk with you about a certification that I'm planning to pursue to make me a more desirable candidate. To be clear, this is not a request for a job interview. I am truly interested in gaining some helpful information and advice.
>
> I am available next Tuesday and Thursday. I promise to take no more than 20 minutes of your time.
>
> Thank you for your consideration.
>
> Sincerely,
>
> Peter Green

Don't become frustrated if you do not get an immediate response. Some people will respond quickly, but many others will take time to respond, while others will need a reminder. If no response within ten days, forward your original email with the following heading and a similar message to the one in the example below:

> Subj: Informational Interview Reminder
>
> Dear John,
>
> I'm not sure if you saw my request for an informational interview, but I will be near your building next Tuesday and Thursday, and would be happy to buy you coffee between 2 and 4pm on either day if you are available. I promise to only take 20 minutes of your time to ask you a few questions and get some advice. If you are too busy, I would appreciate it if you would recommend another successful person at your company with a similar background who might be available to meet with me.
>
> Thanks again.
>
> Peter Green

Just send one reminder. Best not to be seen as a stalker in case the person is just slow to respond. Some people will never respond, but keep in mind that it's a numbers game. The more (well written) requests you send out, the greater number of positive responses you will receive. Some people might say to follow up by phone, but I think it is better to follow up by email to eliminate any chance of miscommunication and to make it easier for the other person to respond.

2- **Prepare for the interview**

- Research the background of the person you will be interviewing on LinkedIn and through a Google search.
- Develop a set of questions as described earlier in this chapter.
- Remember that the person to whom you are talking may be in a position to hire or recommend someone like you for a job in the near future. If so, they want to get to know you as much as they can in 20 or 30 minutes. Be prepared to give your value statement and C.A.R. stories, and answer questions such as why you are interested in his industry.
- Dress professionally, but a little bit more casual than you would for a job interview.
- If there is a chance that you will have coffee or lunch, be prepared to pay.

3- **Hold the interview**

- Arrive at the meeting place 15 minutes early. Spend the time reviewing your research on the interviewee and his company, and looking over your list of questions.
- Remember to be conscious of things that might make a poor impression such as smoking odor (from that last minute cigarette) or gum chewing.

THE POWER OF THE INFORMATIONAL INTERVIEW

- When the other person arrives, greet him with a big smile, strong 6-second handshake with direct eye contact, and thank him for meeting with you.

- If you are in a coffee shop, ask him what he would like to eat or drink as soon as he arrives. Be sure to pay for his order along with yours, even if he insists on paying.

- An informational interview should be thought of as a job interview, except that you are the one who starts the conversation by asking open-ended questions. Begin the conversation by reminding him of your purpose in getting together.

- Ask him friendly questions about his background before asking questions about industries, companies, or jobs.

- Bring your resume along, but don't take it out until he asks to see it. After looking over your resume, he may say something like, "Steven, I'd like to show your resume to my boss (or send it to a friend). Do you happen to have a copy with you?" If this happens, thank him and ask him if he would be willing to make some resume recommendations before he sends it to anyone. If he has time, ask him to take a quick look on the spot. If not, send him your resume by email as soon as you get home. Either way, incorporate his best advice into your resume, and send him an updated resume attached to your thank you email.

- Listen for names of people that he mentions that you might want to ask to be connected to at the end of the conversation, "You mentioned Howard Smith. Is he someone who might give me another perspective?"

- If the interviewee really likes you, and you are near his company's office, he may offer to have you accompany him to his office to meet his boss (maybe a potential hiring manager) before you leave. This is why you will want to suggest meeting near his office. It is also one of the reasons you will want to be well dressed. The other reason is that you don't know how he will be dressed, and you may feel uncomfortable if he is dressed professionally and you are dressed too casually.

- If he does not offer to take your resume to a hiring manager or HR at the end of the interview, tell him that his company sounds great, and ask him if he would be willing to submit your resume to HR or a hiring manager if you see a job on the company website that you feel is an excellent fit. If you have already identified such a job posting, do not mention it since he may feel that this was your only reason for meeting. Send him an email a couple of days later with your resume and a link to the job posting.

- Remember that you only asked for 20 minutes. At the end of that time, thank the person and say that you have used up the promised amount of time, and start to get up to leave. If he is interested in what you have been saying, he may offer to give you some more time to ask a few more questions (a great sign).

- At the end of the interview, thank him for his time and help. If you have thought of a way you might do something for him, mention it. Otherwise, look for ways to repay his kindness in the future.

4- Follow-up After the Interview

Send him a thank you email, such as the one in the following example, within 24-hours. Thank him again for his time and mention how much you enjoyed meeting him. Also, mention how much you appreciate the valuable information and referrals that he provided you, and that you will keep him posted as to your progress. Sign the note "Sincerely," and attach anything that he may have asked you to send him (e.g., resume, portfolio).

THE POWER OF THE INFORMATIONAL INTERVIEW

A hand written note in addition to your email is also acceptable and often appreciated, and should be mailed or dropped off at his office within a day or two of the meeting.

An informational interview may be a one-time event, but it can lead to a mutually beneficial long lasting relationship beyond your job search. Also, keep in mind that if you meet with someone during your Discovery step, you may want to meet with him again when you are in your Action step.

> Subj: Thank You
> Hello Mr Steinfeld,
> Thank you very much for taking the time to meet with me yesterday to discuss developing opportunities in the media industry. I also appreciate your insights and advice, and was very impressed by your knowledge of the new and innovative ways social media is being utilized.
> Thank you also for referring me to John Jones and Jim Smith. I have already contacted Mr Smith at ABC Company, and we expect to meet next week. I plan to contact Mr Jones tomorrow.
> I will be in contact from time to time to keep you posted as to my career exploration and subsequent job search.
> Thanks again for your help.
> Sincerely,
> Lucy Cameron

Common Informational Interview Mistakes

1. Lack of preparation.

2. Arriving late for the interview.

3. Dominating the conversation.

4. Acting too casual or too formal.

5. Wasting time by not staying on topic. You only have 20 minutes, and it goes by quickly. Use it wisely!

6. Mentioning one or more of your weaknesses.

7. Asking unnecessary, closed-ended, or time consuming questions

8. Taking more than the requested amount of time without permission.

9. Asking directly for a job or job interview.

10. Forgetting to ask for additional informational interview referrals.

11. No thank you note (or a poorly written one).

12. Not following up or staying in touch.

Wondering why professionals in your field would be willing to meet you?

10 Reasons You Will Be Granted an Informational (or Job) Interview

1. As a favor for a friend, relative, or another employee.

2. The employee stands to get a referral bonus if he recommends you and you are hired.

3. Your compelling value statement makes him believe that you deserve his help.

4. You mention information or ideas that may be helpful to the hiring manager or the organization.

5. You have common background or interests. These can be work related (work history, clients, acquaintances) or non-work related (culture, sports team affiliation, college).

THE POWER OF THE INFORMATIONAL INTERVIEW

6. He knows about an unannounced staffing need that you might fit. This is what you are hoping for since the company would rather not go through an expensive and lengthy job search process if it can be avoided.

7. He was flattered when you mentioned that you want to talk to him because he is a highly respected person in his industry or company.

8. He loves to give advice and guidance (many professionals do). Using the expression, "I need your help," often leads to a positive result.

9. He is instructed to meet with you by his boss. For example, a very good approach if you do not have a contact in common is to contact a senior executive. If you want to get to the Materials Engineering Manager who works for the Plant Manager, contact the Plant Manager. There is a chance that you will be redirected to a lower level of management, "Thank you for your interest in our company. I suggest that you contact the Materials Engineering Manager." Now, when you email the Materials Engineering Manager, you can honestly say that the Plant Manager suggested you contact him. Even if he does not instruct someone to interview you, there is a good chance that he will refer your resume to the HR department where it may get special attention.

10. He wants to pay forward the help he received when he was searching for a job.

Accept all informational interviews offered, even when you think that they will not provide valuable information or lead to a job offer. You may be surprised by the results. If nothing else, they will give you a great way to practice your interviewing skills.

Mastering Job Interviews

"You never get a second chance to make a first impression."

— Will Rogers, U.S. Humorist

The goal of an in-person interview is to gain insight into your personality, strengths, work behaviors and values, since the interviewer already has a good idea about your skills, knowledge and experience from your resume (and possibly a telephone or Skype interview).

Basic hiring criteria can be expressed in terms of seven words beginning with the letter "C." You should also be looking at these same seven criteria to personally assess your fit for the position.

1. Are you **Competent** to hold the job?
   Do you meet the hiring criteria for this job? If they have brought you in for an interview, they certainly feel that you can probably meet the job requirements, and are hoping that you can exceed the requirements without being overqualified.

2. Are you **Compatible** with the culture of the organization?
   If you are being seriously considered for employment, you are probably perceived as being compatible with the culture (e.g., experienced and highly professional), and able to collaborate effectively with the rest of the organization, but you should independently assess how comfortable you will feel within the culture. It's helpful to look around to get a sense for the diversity, ages and styles of dress of the people you pass on the way in and out of the office.

3. Do you **Communicate** well both verbally and in writing?
   Do not confuse interpersonal skills (ability to get along well with others) with communication skills (the ability to absorb and communicate ideas, both verbally and in writing, across the organization so that other people easily grasp your meaning). Sometimes candidates tell an interviewer that they have great communication skills when they mean interpersonal skills. If your verbal and written communication skills are not strong, you can still do well on the interview if you make the case for employment by virtue of your non-communication related skills and strengths (e.g., technical skills).
   Your ability to hold your own in a **two-way conversation** with the interviewer will be an important indicator of your communication skills.

4. Do you have **Chemistry** with the hiring manager?
   Do you have chemistry with your prospective new boss during the interview? If not, ask why not? If you will be working closely with him, and feel that you will have a hard time forming a working relationship, you may want to seek a different opportunity. Generally speaking, the hiring manager will connect with people in his own image, so you will want to do your best mirror his communication style. For example, if he has an outgoing, strong personality, you may want to talk more, and with more authority, than you would normally.

It is very important to be likeable. A hiring manager will not hire a candidate that he doesn't like, but will hire a candidate he likes very much even if that candidate is lacking in other ways. If he likes you, he will be looking for reasons to hire you. If he doesn't, he will be looking for reasons NOT to hire you. **Make him fall in love with you. If he does, you are almost certain to get a job offer.**

5. Do you have **Confidence** that you can do the job with excellence? No one will hire you if you do not exhibit 100% confidence in your ability to get the job done. If you can only bring one thing with you to a job interview, make it confidence. When talking about yourself, use words like "excellent," "outstanding," and "exceptional." If you have a hard time using those words when describing your strengths and skills, say that other people use those words when describing your skills. In a competitive job market, employers don't hire "good" employees; they hire potentially "great" ones.

6. Will you make a measurable **Contribution?**
Beyond just meeting the basic job responsibilities, will you help the employer meet the goals and challenges of the organization?
Put yourself in the shoes of the hiring manager. He wants to hire achievers who go far beyond their basic job duties to help the company (and his department) achieve its goals (e.g., revenue growth, profitability, cost savings, client and employee satisfaction). Impress the interviewer by delivering prepared C.A.R. stories on how you went above and beyond in the past.
As explained previously, **C.A.R. stands for Challenge, Action, and Result.** Prepare C.A.R. stories that talk about your greatest accomplishments and major strengths, and find a time to comfortably fit them into the conversation. For example, if you are a problem solver, give a C.A.R. story that gives an example of a time you used

that strength. If you have researched the company, include C.A.R. stories that talk about how you helped former employers overcome challenges similar to the ones that the company (or department) is currently facing.

In any case, talk less about challenges and results, and more about your actions. Practice your C.A.R. stories so that you can tell them in less than two minutes. If it is too long, the hiring manager may have a hard time following your story.

> The following is an example of a C.A.R. story:
> **(Challenge)** "Because they were using an outdated survey form, my department was in danger of missing their client satisfaction goals for the year.
> **(Action)** I developed a new, more comprehensive, customer satisfaction survey and contacted our top 50 customers to ask them to quickly complete and return it.
> **(Result)** When we included these surveys in our final results, we had achieved a record high score of 4.5 on a scale of one to five."

Alternate mnemonics to C.A.R. that you may come across that serve the same purpose include S.T.A.R. (Situation, Task, Action, and Result) and S.O.A.R. (Situation, Obstacle, Action, and Result).

7. Are your **Compensation** expectations in line with the budget?
   Do not bring up compensation during an interview. If the interviewer brings it up, just say that you are "flexible" or "open," or "more concerned about finding the right fit." If he insists on getting your salary requirements, mention the range that you have researched, "I understand that the range for this position is between

$65,000 and $75,000." For more on this subject, see the chapter titled *Negotiating Like a Pro*.

Beyond the 7 C's

At the entry level, it is very important to stress your strong work ethic, ability to work well with others, and self-motivation and drive, but one you get to **mid-level positions**, it's more important to stress **problem solving, commitment, time management, accountability, and communication skills**. At the **senior management level**, stress **leadership, strategic thinking, business acumen, high integrity, and global outlook**.

You will want to pay special attention to at least a few of the characteristics listed below. Even though some employers will value some of these attributes as more important than others, none are unimportant, and exhibiting the top three listed below (**passion, enthusiasm, and positive attitude**) will always help your interview. Of course, if you can find out which are most important to the hiring manager through an informational interview, you can focus more attention on those.

Passion

Employers will respond very positively if you mention that you are passionate about your career, mainly because they expect that passionate people will be fully engaged and work very hard.

Enthusiasm

In addition to showing enthusiasm for the position, show enthusiasm for the organization's products or services, mission, vision and goals. As with passion, this will send the message that you plan to work hard. If you need to fake enthusiasm, you may want to look for another opportunity.

Positive Attitude

If an employer had to choose between an employee with an outstanding record but a less than positive attitude and an average employee with an exceptionally positive attitude, he would choose the one with the better attitude. If you arrive at the office in the middle of winter, talk about how you find cold weather invigorating rather than how you had to wait 30 minutes for the bus in the freezing cold.

Global Thinking

This refers to your ability to think across boundaries (department, company, industry, geography) in bringing valuable new ideas to your job or the company. Present yourself as someone constantly seeking better ways to improve results and the work environment.

Integrity and Honesty

These qualities draw people to you and make you an effective leader, team member and mentor.

Determination and Commitment

Get across that you will find a way to achieve and exceed every goal and meet every challenge, despite obstacles put in your way, and you will have an excellent chance of being selected.

Strategic Perspective

This has been identified in surveys of top executives choosing senior management as the single most important characteristic. If you are applying for an executive level job, concentrate on your experience designing successful strategies.

Business Acumen

Overall business judgment is rarely described as a key strength by applicants for leadership positions, although it is highly valued.

Adaptability/Flexibility/Resilience

This refers to your ability to respond quickly and positively to changes in the environment, and your help in creating necessary change. It is especially important that an older candidate exhibit this trait.

Time Management

Express that you do not like to waste time, are always looking for ways to save time (after all, time is money), and that you are also looking for ways to help your fellow employees save time.

Accountability

Show that you take responsibility for your results, including your past failures. You will also want to show that you learned from your mistakes and failures.

Quality

Express that you value quality and want to excel in an organization that values quality (which is one reason you chose to apply to this organization).

Team Playing

A true team player actively pursues the goals of the team regardless of the impact on his own personal interests.

Leadership

Everyone is expected to step up as needed to provide team leadership. Leaders do not have to have a management title. Any employee can lead by setting a positive example, and by driving others to achieve the organization's mission and goals.

Learning

It's particularly important for workers of any age to get across that they are eager to learn, and that can absorb, apply, and communicate new knowledge quickly and effectively with little or no formal training. You can demonstrate your interest in learning by reading at least one recently published book in your field, and finding a good time to reference something from the book during the interview. If the interviewer has also read the book, or has an interest in reading it, it will also help to increase your chemistry with him.

Critical Thinking/Problem Solving

A critical thinker considers facts that are not obvious, actively seeks solutions from others, solves problems creatively, and identifies potential problems. **Problem solving skills are highly valued by all employers.**

Mentorship

If you are good with technology or highly experienced in a specific type of work, mention that you have the capability and willingness to mentor your co-workers who may be having difficulty.

Before the Day of the Interview

Research the Company

You can do this through a Google Advanced Search, on LinkedIn, by reading the latest annual report and press releases, staying on top of what's happening at the company by setting up daily Google Alerts, and through informational interviews.

Research Your Interviewers

Find out as much as you can about your potential interviewers' reputations, personalities, management styles, hobbies, accomplishments, immediate needs, expertise, work histories, and hot button issues. Use Google Advanced Search, LinkedIn, and informational interviews. Make sure that you have the correct spelling of your interviewer's names and current titles.

Take Note of Time and Location

If possible, schedule a time when you are typically at your best (e.g., morning). In any event, schedule the interview on a day or time that will comfortably allow you to arrive near the interview location one hour before the interview.

Double check that you have the correct address of the location where you will be meeting since the company may have multiple offices in the same geography or may have moved recently. Make sure you know how to get there and give yourself extra time in case of transportation or other unexpected delay.

Confirm the Interview

If you have more than one day's notice, send an e-mail to the person who scheduled the interview the day before the interview confirming the day, place, and time. This will not only make you look professional, but may help you avoid an embarrassing or costly mistake if you have written down the wrong day, place, or time.

> Subj: Interview Confirmation
> Dear Ms Jones,
> I am confirming my interview with Mr Steinfeld for tomorrow, June 4th at 3pm at your office on the 19thrd floor of 1440 Illinois Place. If the time or date needs to be rescheduled, or the location changed, please contact me at 555-555-5555.
> I look forward to meeting you when I arrive for the interview.
> Thank you.
> Lucy Cameron

Prepare Your Resume and Portfolio

Prepare five extra copies of your most recently updated resume to take with you, and offer one to everyone who interviews you, "I have a clean copy of my updated resume with me. Would you like a copy?" If you have a portfolio with examples of exemplary work (that's not violating the confidentiality of your former employers), bring it along and find a good time to show it, "Mr Green, Rather than tell you about the ad campaign that I helped put together for Steinfeld Industries, I brought along a copy to show you."

If you are showing your portfolio to demonstrate your creativity, remember to explain how your creativity helped to achieve business goals.

MASTERING JOB INTERVIEWS

Practice Your Answers

Common interview questions, in addition to the ones in this book, can easily be found on the Internet. Be sure to especially practice your answer to the first commonly asked question, "Please tell me about yourself," and your C.A.R. stories until they seem unrehearsed. Your answers should be easy to understand, related to the question, and focused on your accomplishments. Don't memorize your answers, but reduce each one to a few bullet points that you can keep in your head at interviews.

Prepare Your Questions

Prepare the questions that you will ask the interviewer during the course of the interview, paying special attention to the questions that you are expected to ask at the end of the interview. I offer you some good possibilities later in this chapter. **Please keep in mind that if you have no or few questions, the interviewer may think that you are not particularly interested in the job or company.**

Prepare Your Wardrobe

Always have your interview clothing ready to go in case you are called for an interview on short notice. Even if the company has a casual dress policy, dress conservatively in quality clothing for the interview. **It pays to invest in an all-season black, grey or dark blue suit if you are either a man or a woman.** The shirt or blouse that you wear should be solid white or light blue or have a conservative small pattern; and men should wear simple patterned ties in the same color palette as their shirts. Both men and women should wear stylish but conservative leather shoes that match their suit. Men should wear black socks and women should wear neutral pantyhose. It is also very important that your suit and shirt (or blouse) fit you very well. I suggest that you have your suits professionally tailored when you buy them, professionally cleaned and pressed, and your interview shoes kept highly polished and in excellent condition. Women should wear limited amounts of jewelry (of high quality only), make-up and perfume. Men should leave their jewelry (other than a conservative watch and wedding ring) at home.

The Day of the Interview

Stay high energy, but control nervousness. It will help your composure and confidence if you arrive at a local coffee shop near the interview site an hour or more before the interview is scheduled to begin.

When you are settled in at the coffee shop, write down the 3 main selling points you want to make sure you get across at the interview (e.g., proven leadership ability, a track record of sales success, existing relationships with automotive industry customers). Follow this activity by reviewing your research on the company and interviewers, and by taking a final look at the job description. Before leaving the coffee shop, write down a few of your C.A.R. (Challenge, Action and Result) stories in bullet form to anchor positive thoughts. Arrive at the company 15 minutes early for the interview, immediately take off your outerwear and make a quick trip to the rest room to check your appearance.

Put on a smile when you enter the office. Be especially nice to everyone on the way in and out of the office, and engage the receptionist while you are in the reception area. You never know who might comment about you to the interviewer after you leave. "Was Mr Steinfeld here for an interview? I really liked him." If the interviewer is unsure about hiring you or someone else, a positive comment from another person might tip the balance in your favor.

Turn off your cell phone, and when called to enter the office to meet the interviewer, do so without hesitation. Greet the interviewer with a friendly smile, energy, a confident posture with your shoulders back, and direct eye contact. Put down your briefcase or folder, shake the person's hand firmly for six seconds, and sit down at a comfortable distance with your back straight and your knees facing the interviewer.

Ace the Interview

Pay Close Attention to Your Surface Indicators

These include your appearance, personality, attentive listening, and verbal communication skills. Your tone of voice, facial movements and body language are more important than the actual words you say. This is another reason to pursue only jobs that are an excellent fit. **If you want to "sound" genuinely confident and enthusiastic, you need to "be" genuinely confident and enthusiastic.**

Be Genuine

Be yourself, not what you may think the interviewer wants you to be. Any sign of insincerity will create doubt in the mind of the hiring manager about everything you say.

Control Your Nerves

A certain amount of nervous energy can give you a performance edge, but don't allow nervousness to make you fidget or turn you into a robot.

Align Your Value

Talk about your experience selectively. The way to score a winning interview is to align your value with the organization's immediate needs, goals and challenges. This is one of the most important things that you can do on an interview, and why you need to spend whatever time is necessary to research the company completely.

Take Control of the Interview

No matter which question is asked, answer the question but direct your answers as much as possible to what you want to get across to your interviewer (e.g., your 3 main selling points and C.A.R. stories) so that you stand out among the other candidates and are memorable. Think of a politician. When interviewed, a politician will often add several points to his answer that he wants to make sure he gets across even if they are not directly related to the original question.

Be Conversational

Go out of your way to be conversational and show your personality. If you are super friendly or humorous by nature, show it! It will make you more likeable and more memorable.

Keep Your Answers Focused, Short and Direct

When possible, keep your answers under one minute and ALWAYS under two minutes. If you talk any longer, the interviewer may lose interest in what you are saying, you may sound inarticulate, or you may wind up sounding less than confident in your answer.

Always Respond With Positive and Confident Answers

Be positive at all times. This is not the time to be humble or compare your abilities to someone with more experience. **You must make the case that you are an exceptionally strong candidate every minute of the interview.** Do not say something like, "I am very knowledgeable about marketing but wish I knew more about forecasting." Simply say, "I am very knowledgeable about marketing," and stop talking. If you are asked about something that did not work out well, take the opportunity to discuss a turn-around situation in which a poor start ended in a positive outcome.

Actively Listen

Show interest in the interviewer and what he has to say by actively listening much more than you talk. Rephrase and summarize as necessary to understand and clarify questions. Maintain eye contact and be patient.

Watch for Non-Verbal Cues

Is the interviewer leaning forward? If yes, he is interested in what you are saying. Or, is he leaning back with eyes glazing over? Is he sitting in an open, receptive position or sitting with his shoulder turned toward you or with his arms folded and feet crossed? If you are getting negative cues, you may want to shorten your answers and start asking questions to engage the interviewer.

Know Your Resume Well

They were impressed enough with your resume to ask you to interview. The interviewer's questions will let you know what stood out. Be very familiar with every line in your resume, and anticipate possible questions.

Summarize the Meeting

Start with expressing your interest and enthusiasm for both the company and position, followed by how you can contribute to meeting the goals or challenges of the organization, "Thank you for meeting with me today. I'm not only excited about the job, but impressed by what you've told me about the organization's plans. I hope you agree that my experience and detail orientation can help contribute to your development of an improved accounting system."

Non-Traditional In-Person Interviews

When we think of interviewing, we naturally think of a traditional one-on-one interview with the hiring manager or a series of in-person interviews leading up to the final decision maker; but there are a growing number of different types of interviews that you may be exposed to during your career. The key is to basically handle them in the same way as you would a traditional interview, but with an awareness of the differences explained below.

Panel or Group Interviews

Don't get nervous if there is more than one interviewer in the room. This could signal insecurity in any one individual's interviewing ability, the need to save time in the interviewing process, or wanting to come to a quick consensus, "I liked Lucy. What did you guys think of her? Do we agree that she is one of our top candidates?" Focus on making sure that you address each person in the group, keep your answers short and to the point so as not to lose anyone's interest, and spend more time making eye contact with the key decision makers. Some group interviews are meant to be "stress interviews" where your composure and confidence are under examination, so be sure to keep your cool.

Informal Interviews

If you get invited to a lunch or coffee, order the same thing that the interviewer orders (or something at similar cost), avoid alcoholic beverages, and stay very mindful of your table manners. Don't lower your guard because of the informal atmosphere. Give the same answers that you would give in a more formal environment.

Telephone and Skype Interviews

Prior to an in-person interview, you may be asked to participate in a telephone interview. This type of interview is typically led by an HR professional in a large company, and a hiring manager in a small company.

The purpose is to reduce the number of candidates invited to meet with the management team in person.

Although you may get a few behavioral questions in a telephone interview, you can expect it to be mainly focused on the facts contained in your resume. Since the interview will only be scheduled for 20 or 30 minutes, you will need to be well prepared to answer questions with little hesitation. Give this interview the same weight as an in-person interview. Keep in mind that you will not be taking the next step if you are not one of the top candidates after all their telephone interviews are completed.

They have asked you to the telephone interview because they suspect that you have the background needed to be successful—but you will be expected to build a strong case for being hired—and defend and expand on every accomplishment bullet in your resume.

Preparing for a Telephone Interview

Keep the following within easy reach:

- Your resume

- Company research

- Your C.A.R. stories (in bullet form)

- The job posting. Mark it up in green, yellow, and red as discussed in the chapter titled The 3 Steps. Pay special attention to where you are strongest and weakest. Bring the conversation back to your strongest qualifications as often as possible and do not mention your weaknesses.

- Your 3 main selling points. The same interviewers may be conducting several telephone interviews in a row, and you want them to remember you when they get together to discuss who will be selected for an in-person interview ("Lucy Cameron? I remember her well. She was the one who is passionate about marketing communications, received certification in social media, and won an award at Steinfeld Industries for developing a very creative promotional campaign.")

- Written answers (in bullet form) to questions about your resume, skills, strengths, and background that you might expect to receive

- Questions to ask the interviewer (see examples later in this chapter)

Telephone Interview Tips
These tips are in addition to the basic interview tips shared later in this chapter

- When first contacted, ask for an in-person interview if the interviewer is in your same city. They may turn you down, but it's worth a try.

- If you are called without warning, even if you are available, explain that it is an inconvenient time, and schedule a time later in the day or the next day when you will be prepared.

- Be aware of possible time differences. If the caller is in New York City, but you are in Chicago, the time of the interview will be different in each city.

- Take the call from a private, quiet location. Avoid public spaces.

- Try to take the call on a land line rather than your cell phone so there is less chance of being disconnected. Stand or walk around during the entire interview (this will give you both energy and a stronger voice).

- Remember to smile during the call.

- Be careful not to interrupt the interviewer.

- Speak clearly, confidently, and slowly—and don't allow your voice to trail off or rise at the end of a sentence. No matter how slowly you think you are speaking, you will be speaking more quickly than you think. Speak especially slowly when mentioning something very important that you want to get across.

- Do your best to put your complete and focused attention on what the interviewer is saying rather than focusing on your prepared materials.

Phone Interview Questions

The following are examples of questions you may get on a phone interview. Although you may be asked some of the same behavioral questions asked at an in-person interview, there will be more questions focused on your resume, your understanding of the job, and your ability to do the job with excellence. **You will also probably get most of the same questions on a Skype interview that you will get on a telephone interview.**

- Tell me about your education, training, skills, strengths and experience as it relates to this job.

- Tell me what you did at (ABC) company?

- Tell me about a time that you participated in a team. What was your role?
- Why do you think you will be successful at this job?
- What do you know about our company?
- What type of work environment do you prefer?
- What requirements of this job are you unsure or less confident about?

Skype Interviews

Many companies are moving from phone to Skype interviews in order to simulate more of an in-person interview experience. Prepare for a Skype interview in much the same way that you would an in-person interview, while utilizing the tips below:

- Since you will be visible to the interviewer, place your most important bulleted points (including the 3 main selling points you want them to remember about you) onto Post-It Notes around your screen, but only glance at them when absolutely necessary since you will want to keep steady eye contact into the camera as much as possible. This will require you to prepare much more for a Skype interview than one by telephone, and only slightly less than necessary for an in-person interview.
- Dress business casual in muted colors, and pay special attention to your grooming.

- When preparing for the interview, choose your location carefully. Set up a Skype call in advance with a friend to practice and help set your camera's positioning in the room. Use a private room with good lighting, and make sure that the interviewer is not going to be distracted by anything in the background, including pets.

- If you might be disturbed, place a "Do Not Disturb – Interview in Progress" sign on the door.

- Sit at a desk or table. Check your Internet connection.

- Turn off any other programs running on your computer so you don't get distracted if an email suddenly pops up while you are speaking.

- Speak CLEARLY and SLOWLY into the microphone.

- Make sure that you have a phone number and/or email for the main interviewer, so you can contact him if you run into any technical issues.

- At the end of the interview, wait for the other party to log off, and double check that you are logged off before you get up from your chair.

In-Person Interview Q's and A's

You should always be prepared to answer questions that are very specific to the job, particularly if you are interviewing with the hiring manager. However, you also need to prepare for common open-ended questions that are important to all interviewers. Below are a dozen questions that are commonly asked in one form or another. Some of these are behavioral questions meant to uncover how you acted in specific situations in the past. The logic is that past performance is likely to be repeated in the future. I have included the interviewer's probable thinking behind the questions (shown in parentheses).

Whenever possible, **direct your answer to one of your 3 main selling points or C.A.R. stories** that support your strengths and accomplishments.

Q1. **Please tell me about yourself** (Why are you qualified for this job. Focus on highlights from your resume and insights into your character that I can't get from your resume).
A. **This is often the first question asked and your answer will set the tone for the entire interview.**

The interviewer is not looking for a rehash of the basic information in your resume. He is looking for a summary of the reasons he should consider hiring you—and is also testing your verbal communication skills.

You can answer this important question by following the sample format below:

"**I'm a** (marketing professional) **with a passion for** (rodeo marketing). **I chose** (marketing) **as a career because I have always had an interest in** (consumer behavior). **I am strong at** (creating compelling advertising campaigns), **and have often been told that I have excellent** (teamwork and problem solving skills). **I demonstrated all my strengths and skills at** (three of the top companies in the rodeo advertising industry where I was consistently given increasing responsibility). **I also** (play golf at a relatively high level). **I bring the same** (competitiveness and commitment to excellence) **to everything I do.**"

Q2. **Why are you interested in working for this company?** (Are you applying to a million companies or are you being selective? Also, convince me that you've researched us).
A. Do not make meaningless statements such as "I want to work for a big company." Instead say something like, "I've been engaged in both marketing and the financial services industry for much of my career. I've

researched this company both online and through informational interviews with two of your current employees. I believe that your goals and team-oriented culture fit well with the type of job and organization where I can fit in well and make an immediate contribution. For example, I found out that you are expanding your social networking presence. I'm 100% confident that I can contribute to developing and implementing your next generation applications."

Q3. What are your greatest strengths? (Show me you have the soft skills necessary to be successful at this particular job).
A. "I have been told that my top strengths are my analytical, problem solving, and written communication skills. I believe that my ability to build strong client relationships is one of my greatest strengths.

Q4. What would you say is your number one weakness? (Everyone has weaknesses. Tell me about one that can negatively affect the quality of your work or your productivity. Tell me how you are working to make it less of a problem).
A. **If you actually talk about a real weakness, it may be all the interviewer remembers at the end of the interview.** Instead, give a short answer about how you sometimes overuse one of your strengths and mention that you have worked to overcome that challenge, "One of my greatest strengths is my attention to detail. However, sometimes I spend too much time checking for errors. This is something I have been working hard to change. Instead of checking my results three or four times, I am getting to the point where I only check it once or twice."

Q5. Why did you leave your last job? (Was there a problem?)
A. Give a simple answer such as, "I was laid off from my position as a loan officer due to the recession. If you are currently employed, say something along the lines of, "I've worked hard to prepare myself to get to the next

level, but there are limited opportunities for advancement at my current company."

Q6. Please tell me about a difficult challenge you faced at work, and how you handled it (Give me a C.A.R. story about one of your greatest accomplishments. Keep in mind that I am also interested in understanding what you consider to be a "difficult" challenge).
A. "At my last company, I was given the challenge to analyze the social media strategy of the company's competitors. I executed an in-depth analysis of the company's top five competitors, and was very proud when they decided to use my results as the basis for new revenue generating social media campaign."

Q7. Tell me about a failure or major mistake you've made in your career (Do you learn from your mistakes and can you quickly recover from them? Do you take responsibility for failure or blame someone or something else?)
A. "When I was a new marketing associate, my department failed in meeting a project goal on time. I learned something about time management from that experience that I have never forgotten, and even though I had just joined the company, I took my share of the responsibility along with the rest of the team."

Q8. What do you think you will be doing five years from now? (Do you have realistic expectations? Do you see yourself still working for our company?)
A. Give the interviewer the impression that you plan to be with the company for the long haul, and that you have no plans to retire, "It's difficult to look that far ahead, but this appears to be a great company. I would hope to be working here for the rest of my career. I don't know what my job title would be in five years, but would expect to be taking on a lot more responsibility by that time."

Q9. Why have you had three jobs in the last six years? (Are you a job hopper?)

A. In general, I recommend that you are as honest as possible in this situation while making sure to list your accomplishments in each role. **Keep it positive, and avoid appearing to be disgruntled or arrogant.** Good reasons for job changes include: a chance for more responsibility or the opportunity to work for an exciting start-up company where the company was ultimately not successful. Saying that you were laid off due to a restructuring that eliminated entire departments is also a good reason. If asked if you were fired from a job, explain that the company's culture was not a good fit and that you left by mutual agreement. **Keep in mind that a candidate who may be perceived as a "job hopper" is much more likely to land an interview as the result of a recommendation to the hiring manager,** "Joe, You really should take a look at Steven Steinfeld. He's made a few career choices in the past five years that didn't work out, but I think he would be a great fit for the opening in our company."

Q10. Tell me about a time when you had to communicate with someone may not have personally liked you. How did you handle it? (Do you have strong inter-personal skills?)

A. "People usually like me, but I understand that you don't always have the same chemistry with everyone. If I suspect that someone has less than a great opinion of me, for whatever reason, I go out of my way to be especially friendly and supportive."

Q11. How would you describe your leadership style? (Why do people follow your lead?)

A. "I believe in leading by example. I also believe in building strong teamwork by being inclusive and respectful of all suggestions and recommendations. Even when I have not been in a formal leadership position, I have often provided leadership to my team."

Q12. Why should we hire you rather than one of our other excellent candidates? What's special about you? (I don't want to make a mistake, so help me justify hiring you to my senior management. Tell me in not too many words why you are exceptionally suited for this job).

A. This is often the last question asked, and may represent your last chance to summarize your case for being hired. "Based upon what I know about the job, I believe that I have an excellent mix of strengths, skills, and knowledge to do an outstanding job. I don't know how good your other candidates are with your accounting software and Excel, but I am outstanding at both. I also believe that my enthusiasm for the company and the position will show up in my commitment to doing the best job possible. As a start, I believe that I can make an immediate contribution to setting up the new reporting structure that you mentioned."

Interview Questions Testing Critical Thinking Ability

Usually critical thinking is tested only during technical interviews, but sometimes the interviewer may test your critical thinking during a non-technical interview. There is almost no limit to the number of questions that can be asked to test your problem solving ability. One popular one is, "If you were an ingredient in a Big Mac, which ingredient would you be?" Before answering, you will quickly need to decide whether you see yourself as the meat (of the organization) or the bun that holds everything together. Or maybe you see yourself as the sauce that makes it special.

Here are three rules of thumb to keep in mind when answering, since the answer is less important than the thought process:

You've been given everything you need to give an answer. Don't ask for more information.

Speak your thoughts out loud so that the interviewer can hear the process you are using the try to find the answer.

Sometimes the best answer is to say "I would do a Google search."

Questions to Ask the Interviewer

Selecting meaningful questions to ask is often the most difficult part of the interview. You can overcome this, and stand out from other candidates, if you prepare questions to ask in advance.

You don't need to wait to the end of the interview to ask questions, but the interviewer will always ask you if you have any questions before ending the interview, "Do you have any questions for me?" Interviewers will actually appreciate questions at any point in the interview if they are not very experienced at interviewing and are struggling to find questions to ask you.

Don't ask more than 3 questions in a row, and **don't ask questions that make it appear that you are more concerned with what you want from the job** (e.g., experience, knowledge, a high salary, or training) **than making a contribution to the goals of the organization.**

Don't ask questions such as "What will I be doing in a typical day?" or "What is my work schedule?" or "What do you expect of me?" **Your questions should demonstrate that you are focused on adding value rather than on routine activities.** Also, do not ask questions about the organization that you could have gotten easily from the company website or that ask about the company's high level strategy. **Keep to questions that show that you are focused on the job and needs of the department under discussion.**

The following are types of other questions that I often hear at interviews that are NOT particularly helpful to leaving the best impression:

- How do you like working for the company? (Leave this type of question for informational interviews).
- How do I fit into the organization? (You should be telling the interviewer, not asking)

> - What training and development programs do you offer? (Save this for after you accept the job offer since you should be focused on explaining what you can do now)
>
> - Why is this position open? (Assume that the last person did not work out. You will find out why later. If it is a new position, the interviewer will explain why it has been created.)
>
> - Please rate me with other candidates on a scale of 1-10 (You can ask how you compare to other candidates he has seen, but do not put him on the spot by asking for a number. In any event, he will not give you one).

Below are ten good questions that you might consider using at an in-person job interview. Select four to six of them, ensuring that you include number 9.

Questions to Ask the Interviewer

1. What are the 3 top criteria you are looking for in a candidate? If possible, ask this early in the interview. If you can start the conversation by asking the interviewer to explain the most important success factors in the job under discussion, you will have a huge advantage since you will be able to tailor your answers to his criteria. If he responds that this was laid out in the job description, tell him that you are familiar with the job description but that you would like his personal viewpoint.

2. Can you please describe the culture of the organization? What type of person is happiest and most successful working here?

3. What are the department's immediate goals and challenges?

4. What would you like me to accomplish in my first month? First 3 to 6 months? What about long term?

5. I'm an excellent problem solver. It there an immediate situation where I could add some value?

6. Ask at least one question that shows that you have researched the company (e.g., I have been researching your company online, and have a question about your social media strategy).

7. From everything that I went over, do think you that I'm the employee you're looking for? This will allow you one last chance to clear up any misunderstandings and restate your case for employment if necessary. His answer might also help you do better in your next interview.

8. Do you have any concerns that I need to clear up in order to be your top candidate?

9. I am very excited about the organization and the job. What are the next steps in the interview process?

10. What is the best way to follow up with you?

20 Interviewing Tips

1. Be yourself. If you call yourself Bob or Rob, don't introduce yourself as Robert.

2. Call the interviewer by his first name if at all comfortable. If not use Mr or Ms, not Sir or Madam.

3. Keep your hands away from your face and your mouth, and avoid excessive gesturing.

4. Do not remain overly soft spoken or quiet out of respect for the interviewer. It may come across as a lack of confidence.

5. Don't use the word "We" too often unless you are interviewing at a non-profit. Companies are interested in what you did more than what the team accomplished. Use the word "I" as much as possible.

6. Avoid apologizing or being defensive about things you can't change (e.g., age, education, or specific experience).

7. Don't take notes, except to write down important names and positions that may come up during the interview on a small pad.

8. Don't mention part-time jobs that you plan to keep (e.g., weekend real estate sales or family business).

9. Don't look at your watch during the interview, even if you are curious as to the time. You may appear to be bored or disinterested.

10. Be sure to collect the business cards of everyone you meet and record them in a PC spreadsheet or phone app when you get home.

11. Make every word count. Avoid using filler words such as "like," "umm," or "you know."

12. Give the interviewer time to reflect on what you are saying.

13. If your interviewer is speaking very quickly, do NOT speed up. Instead, shorten your answers to help increase the pace of conversation.

14. Avoid discussing politics or other subjects that might be controversial. If the interviewer brings uncomfortable subjects up during small talk at the beginning of the interview, change the subject.

15. If the interviewer asks you a sensitive question that you think is inappropriate (e.g., marital status, physical disabilities), respond with "Is this relevant to the position?" He will likely withdraw the question.

16. When talking to the hiring manager, stress your drive and ambition but be careful not to give the impression that you will be disappointed if the job under discussion does not lead to bigger and better things in the very near future.

17. Listen carefully to the questions so that you do not give the wrong answer. For instance, if he asks you to give an example of a project you did at your last job, be sure not to give an example of a project you did two jobs ago. If unsure of the question, ask for clarification.

18. If you have something negative in your background that is likely to come up during a pre-employment check (e.g., credit issues, criminal conviction), come clean during the final interview. Have a good explanation ready that explains the circumstances in the most positive light possible, and explain how you have been going about fixing or moving on from the problem. Move the conversation back quickly to explaining why you are a strong candidate for the job.

19. At the end of the conversation, mention important qualifications that may not have been touched upon. They may very well have been contained in your cover letter, but your cover letter may not have been read, "It's not in resume, but I think it's important to mention that growing up on a farm will help me be successful in a marketing position working with clients and data in the agriculture industry."

> 20. **Mention something that makes you memorable. SHOW YOUR PERSONALITY** (e.g., likeable, charming, funny), and build a clear case for why you should be hired among all candidates. At the end of a day of interviewing several candidates; only the ones who have stood out, will be remembered. Be one of them! "Lucy Cameron? I remember her well. When we spoke about her interest in marathon running, I was impressed by her competitiveness, and when I asked her what her biggest weakness is, she said "chocolate."

Especially Important Tips for Older Interviewees

Anticipating stereotyping, and knowing how to handle it, is one of the keys to mastering the job interview since it will surely come into play if you are over 50 years old.

The key to handing age stereotypes is to exhibit the characteristics exhibited by young employees as much as possible. These include:

> - Physically able, healthy
> - Easy to supervise and train
> - Flexible
> - Satisfied at lower compensation levels
> - Comfortable with technology and social networking
> - Creative
> - High energy
> - Motivated to take initiative
> - Willing to endure long hours

- Able to multi-task

- Connect easily with younger colleagues, customers, vendors, clients, investors, or funders

You also need to remember the following:

Appearance Counts Even More

If you are a woman who has not updated her hair style since middle school, this may be a good time for a change. If you are a man, don't wear the suit that you wore to your son's graduation ten years ago, get a new one, and match it with a blue or striped shirt and fashionable tie. You do not need to look young, but you do need to look modern.

Forget About Age

If the hiring manager is determined to hire a 25 year-old and you're 55, there is nothing you can do to compensate—so why worry about it? Go into the interview with the attitude that he is looking for a seasoned, mature professional. Forget about the age of the interviewer who may remind you of your son or daughter. Just be sure you don't talk to him as you would one of your children, or the way you might treat a student or protégé. Forget about age discrimination. It is very difficult to prove, so don't go into the interview looking for it.

Forget About Your Weaknesses

If being highly prolific in technology is an absolute job requirement, and you can't use a basic word processing program, there is little you can do about that on the day of the interview. Bring every question back to your strengths. Workers are typically hired for their strengths, especially if they can align their value with an immediate organizational need. **If you can align your value better than other candidates, they won't care about your weaknesses OR your age!**

Avoid Tricky Work vs. Life Questions

I am speaking about the ones that might lead to volunteering personal information that can work against you. A common example for older women, in particular, would be questions trying to uncover whether you must care for an aging parent. Answer any question about working overtime or on weekends with, "No problem. I expect that to happen on occasion. I also have no problem with bringing work home if necessary to meet important deadlines."

Get Across that you are a Fast Learner

Fit in at least one example prepared that demonstrates that you learn very quickly, "I didn't know how to use Microsoft Access when I started my last job, but I was able to become skilled within a month or so by spending time with tutorials and experimenting with applications after work. I expect I can do the same with any new program." This will come in particularly handy if you are asked about a required or desired skill that you don't currently possess. By the way, you can download and practice with a free trial copy of the latest Microsoft Office release from www.microsoft.com.

After the Interview

As soon as the interview is over, go back to the original coffee shop or other nearby location to write down what you think went well during every stage of the interview, and what you can improve for the next interview. Keep in mind that if the interview did not go well, it may not be due to anything you said or did. Once you think it over, you might decide that you were not really interested in the job or the company.

You can use the following check list to evaluate how you did, and take notes on how to improve for the next interview:

My Non-Verbal Communication
_ I maintained eye contact
_ I used positive body language
_ I consistently showed enthusiasm and energy
_ I did not fidget or otherwise show nervousness
_ I was appropriately dressed

Verbal Communication
_ I avoided filler words such as Umm
_ I spoke slowly and provided clear responses to questions
_ I emphasized my strengths and highlighted my top skills
_ I used proper grammar and avoided using acronyms
_ I provided specific examples of my accomplishments and strengths with C.A.R. stories
_ I paused to organize my thoughts prior to responding to difficult questions
_ I kept all of my answers under 2 minutes

Also
_ I remained positive throughout
_ I showed self-confidence
_ I expressed well defined career goals
_ I showed my personality (e.g., likeable, charming, funny)
_ I had good chemistry with the interviewer
_ My answers were consistent
_ I finished strong (summarized my case, expressed my enthusiasm for the job and the company, and sold myself as an outstanding candidate)
_ I demonstrated that I researched the organization
_ I asked good questions at the end including asking about next steps

> For my next interview, I should focus on improving:
> 1-
> 2-
> 3-

Following Up With a Thank You Note in Writing

A handwritten thank you note (with good penmanship on fine stationery) is optional after an interview, but a thank you email should always be sent for the simple reason that a hand written note will not allow you to write everything that needs to be communicated:

- Your enthusiasm for the company and job
- A piece of information that you wish you had mentioned (or elaborate on an important interview answer that could have been improved)
- Your knowledge of the company and at least one contribution you can make
- Your past successes that align with the company's challenges or goals
- Work samples (if very relevant to your conversation)
- Contact information for your references (only if requested)
- If following up to a telephone or Skype interview, be sure to mention that you look forward to meeting the interviewer in person

Send your thank you email within 24 hours. I recommend you write it as soon as you return home from the interview, but don't send it until the following morning. Your brain will continue working on the note even while you sleep, and you are sure to improve it if you take some time between your draft and the final version. Proofread it

MASTERING JOB INTERVIEWS

multiple times before sending it to make sure that your English grammar and spelling are correct and that you are not using slang. If you are not totally confident in your grammar, keep your note short, and make an effort to have someone with excellent writing skills quickly proofread and edit it.

Address the interviewer formally even if you addressed him by his first name at the interview, followed by three relatively short paragraphs.

The first paragraph should include the job title and thank him for his time. You might continue by remarking on an interesting exchange that you had during the interview to help him remember how much he liked you. If there is something important that you wish you had pointed out during the interview, you can also mention it at the end of this first paragraph, "By the way, after the interview, I realized that I should have mentioned the fact that I will complete Advanced Excel training next month."

The second paragraph should remind the interviewer why you believe that you are a strong candidate. Be sure to connect your potential contribution with information about the company's immediate needs or longer term challenges or goals.

The last paragraph should talk about your enthusiasm for the opportunity, and indicate when and how you are going to follow up.

Subj: Thank You

Hello Mr Steinfeld,

Thank you for taking the time to interview me yesterday for the position of Marketing Manager. I enjoyed our conversation, particularly the part where we discussed how social media marketing has been exploding over the last few years.

I would like to take this opportunity to highlight three points that we discussed that make me a strong candidate for the position:

> 1. I know what it takes to effectively lead all aspects of weekly retail sales reporting.
> 2. You mentioned the importance of data analysis. This is one of my greatest skills.
> 3. You also mentioned competitive snapshots and pricing assessments. I have conducted competitive analysis and price point comparison projects in each of my last two positions.
>
> As discussed, I will follow up with you for a status next week. In the interim, please feel free to contact me if you need additional information. You can reach me at 555-555-5555.
>
> Thank you again for considering me for this opportunity. I am very excited about the possibility of joining your team.
>
> Sincerely,
>
> Lucy Cameron

If you were at a panel interview (several of them and one of you), write the thank you to the person who will be your direct supervisor and .cc everyone else who was there. If there were multiple but separate interviews, you can do the same, or write a note to each interviewer. If you decide to write separate notes, they should all be slightly different. For example, you might change the sentence where you talk about an interesting exchange you had during the interview.

Following Up by Phone

Although an email is standard practice, make a thank you phone call instead if you are uncomfortable with your writing ability and have no one to review and edit your note. Leave a very short and upbeat message, **before or after normal business hours**, expressing thanks for the time spent interviewing you, and how much you are looking forward to taking the next step. You have only 30 seconds to leave this message, but that should not be a problem. In any event, write down and practice what you are going to say until you can comfortably deliver the message without sounding as if you are reading it. Time the length of your call so that you are not concerned that you may exceed 30 seconds. **Talk very slowly and clearly.** If you make a mistake, opt out of voicemail and re-record the message until you are satisfied. Remember to leave a number where you can be reached at the end of the call.

"Hi Mr Steinfeld, This is Lucy Cameron. I am calling to thank you for taking the time to interview me yesterday. I am very excited about the opportunity, and am looking forward to taking the next step. If you have any additional questions, I can be reached at 555-555-5555. Thank you again."

Decision Day

If you were told that there would be a decision on a certain day, "We will be making a decision by Monday," assume that you will get their decision within a few days of that date.

If you don't hear from him after two weeks from the promised decision date (or from the interview date if there was no decision date given), send a friendly email without mentioning that they are beyond the promised decision date. Use a simple subject line that will result in the email being opened.

> Subj: Marketing Analyst Interview
> Hello Mr Steinfeld,
> Thank you again for the time you spent interviewing me for a Marketing Analyst position two weeks ago. I am writing to find out the status of your decision and to let you know of my continued interest and enthusiasm for both the position and the company.

> If I do not hear from you soon, I will assume that the position has been filled. If that is the case, I hope that you will consider me for a similar position in the near future.
> I hope to hear from you soon. I can be reached at 555-555-5555.
> Thank you.
> Lucy Cameron

If you still do not hear from them, they may have offered the job to another candidate. If that is the case, you may hear from them if they can't come to terms with that person. In any event, stalking them for an answer will only make you seem desperate, and **desperate candidates don't get hired.** Trust that they have not forgotten about you. Common courtesy says that they should inform you that you have not been selected, but you may never be notified. **While you are waiting for a decision — even if you feel confident that we will be receiving a job offer — do not slow down your job searching activities.** Always assume that you have not been selected, and keep moving on to new opportunities.

Q. How do I find out why I didn't get the job?
A. You probably don't find out since the company has nothing to gain by sharing that information. There are many good reasons that you were not selected even if you were an outstanding candidate, so **while it is normal to be very disappointed, there is no reason to get discouraged.** It might have been as simple as you were not available to start as soon as needed or the position was put on hold. Here are some other possibilities:

Why You Were Not Offered the Job

1. You did not follow up. When I ask job candidates why they didn't follow up, answers include, "They should be contacting me," and

MASTERING JOB INTERVIEWS

"I'd rather postpone the bad news." Following up is critical, and shows that you care. If you did not follow up, the employer might have questioned your level of interest in the job and/or the company.

2. There was a more attractive candidate — maybe someone who may not have been as talented as you, but was better able to sell himself, or came highly recommended (a good possibility).

3. You did not have excellent chemistry with the interviewer.

4. Someone who did not meet with you made the final decision.

5. You said something on the way out that was a turn-off to the interviewer. Don't let your guard down for a second until after you leave the building.

6. At least one of your references did not give you a strong recommendation.

7. LinkedIn, Facebook, or Google gave negative information about you or did not match with what you said on your resume or at your interview.

8. You did not show enough enthusiasm for the company or the job.

9. You need more interviewing practice.

Q. I might not have gotten the job, but how do I know if I did well on the interview?
A. Ask yourself if the interviewer seemed genuinely interested in your answers and was selling you on the company during the interview. If he wasn't, the interview probably did not go as well as you thought. The same is true for the amount of time spent in the interview. Even if the interview does not go well, you will probably be given about 15 minutes to make

your case. The more time beyond those 15 minutes, the better it probably went.

Q. Should I turn down interviews for jobs of little interest?
A. **Never turn down a phone or any other type of interview** since it will be great practice for when it matters. In addition, there are 3 other great reasons to interview whenever you can:

1. If you do very well on the interview, you may also be offered a better job than the one for which you are interviewing.

2. It may give you some bargaining power during another interview if you are asked if you are interviewing elsewhere.

3. While the company is interviewing you, you are also interviewing the company. The more you interview, the easier it will be for you to evaluate an opportunity against other potential opportunities.

Non-Profit Work

"Do well by doing good."
— Benjamin Franklin

Although non-profit work is often thought of as being better attuned to younger workers who may be more idealistic and willing to work for less compensation, it is an avenue that should not be discounted by professionals coming out of the for-profit environment. Non-profit organizations are relatively insensitive to age and appreciative of corporate experience and transferable skills (e.g., marketing, sales or finance).

If you are coming out of the for-profit world, it's important to understand that non-profit work is neither an escape from the pressures of the corporate world nor an escape from office politics. For the most part, the pressure can be just as intense as in the for-profit world. Much of the pressure can come from the relative lack of resources available to non-profits to achieve their goals. Other differences include being managed by a Board of Directors (having many bosses as opposed to one) and management by consensus (volunteers and staff are empowered).

Q. What do I need to be aware of before approaching a non-profit?
A. Saying that you want to "do good," "give back," or "make a positive impact," will not be seen as defining reasons for you to be hired for a job

in the non-profit sector. The hiring manager will be interested in the following:

1. **Competency**—Stress your transferable skills, especially the ones that align with the mission and challenges of the organization, and your ability to multi-task.
2. **Strengths in Collaboration** and **Consensus** building. In the non-profit world, it's often a collegial environment where "We" is more often spoken than "I." On an interview, you should talk about your personal accomplishments, but you should stress how those accomplishments supported successful team efforts
3. **Capacity Building** and other nomenclature used in non-profit work
4. **Compensation** (satisfaction with compensation that is often lower than for similar work at a for profit organization)
5. **Passion for the Mission of the organization**
6. **Experience with the non-profit Culture**

Q. How do I know which organizations to approach?
A. A good way to get familiar with the mission and culture of a non-profit is to volunteer. Start by researching an organization through volunteermatch.com, guidestar.org and informational interviews.

Q. Are there other qualities that are particularly important to non-profit organizations?
A. Since non-profit employees often wear many hats, do more with less, and have little opportunity for in-house training, they need their employees to be self-sufficient, flexible, versatile and adaptive, quick learners, and have good Microsoft Office skills.

NON-PROFIT WORK

Q. Is that it?

A. No. You will also need to convince the hiring manager that you will have longevity with the organization. Longevity is very important to a non-profit because relationships are critical. If a non-profit experiences high staff turnover, donors may lessen their contributions, and it will be more difficult to establish other necessary bonds within the community. Employees who come from the for-profit world that wind up leaving non-profits do so because of their frustration with the realities of non-profit culture and finances, especially the slow decision making process. If someone has no record of working or volunteering at a non-profit, she will find that hiring managers are extremely skeptical of her candidacy. The best way to overcome this skepticism is to demonstrate commitment to the mission and values of the organization by offering to start as a volunteer or intern.

Volunteer Strategically

"The best way to find yourself is to lose yourself in the service of others"

- Mahatma Gandhi

No matter how long you have been in transition, start volunteering as soon as possible — but **volunteer strategically**. If dogs are your passion, and you are pursuing a marketing career, don't volunteer to clean cages at the local pet shelter, volunteer to help with their promotional or event planning activities. If you are an accountant, volunteer to help them with their books or tax preparation. If you are in sales, volunteer to help with fund raising..... You get the idea! Check out websites such as volunteermatch.com to find assignments that match you interests, career goals, and time availability.

There are at least five great reasons to volunteer:

1. It gives you the chance to gain experience, sharpen your skills, and learn new skills.

2. Community service work looks impressive on your resume, particularly if it demonstrates important strengths such as collaboration, leadership, or program management.

3. Volunteering provides a great opportunity to network. In a non-profit environment, you not only have the chance to mix with volunteers, but you may have the opportunity to network with staff, the Board of Directors, and corporate donors. You may also have the opportunity to meet important contacts at non-profit social events (you can offer to work as a volunteer at these events even if you have never volunteered at the organization in the past).

4. Volunteering helps build confidence and sense of community that contribute toward maintaining a positive mind-set during a sometimes frustrating job search.

5. If your goal is to pursue a non-profit job, it will give you the credentials and understanding of the non-profit culture required to be considered for employment.

Working with 3rd Parties and References

"Depend on yourself and you will never be let down."
<u>Madhuri Dixit</u>- Indian Bollywood Actress

In this chapter, when I say 3rd parties, I am mostly referring to recruiters who do not work directly for an employer. These recruiters, who typically work on a "contingency" basis, seek out and provide job candidates to their client companies, but receive no payment from these companies unless their candidates are hired. Relationships with these recruiters may expand your opportunities, particularly for contract positions.

The recruiter may find you on LinkedIn or other social media, or you can do some research to find a recruiter who specializes in your field. In any event, **do not depend on a 3rd party recruiter to take responsibility for your job search,** particularly since he may never bring you to the attention of a company if you are not one of his most qualified candidates. Also be aware that 3rd party recruiters are typically more interested in finding candidates for full time positions who are currently employed (known as passive candidates), since that is the greatest value-add that they can provide to an employer. A recruiter may also just be building his database with your resume without having an immediate opportunity. Keep in mind always that a recruiter works for his clients to help them find qualified candidates for specific jobs. **His job is not to find a job for you!**

In many cases, the recruiter will lead you to a contract assignment. **If you receive an offer for a contract assignment through a 3rd party, you need to know who will be your employer of record.**

Other 3rd parties that can positively impact your job search are one-to-one job search coaching and non-profit transitional career coaching, resume development, and job placement services, but enter into these relationships with a detailed understanding of the services offered and the costs.

Tips on Working with 3Rd Party Recruiters

- Check the reputation and references of these individuals and organizations before entering into a relationship.

- Do not pay the recruiter. He will be paid by the hiring company if you are hired and stay for a specific amount of time (e.g., 3 months).

- Do not provide sensitive information (e.g., social security number) or sign agreements that you have not had carefully reviewed (preferably by an attorney).

- Be honest with the recruiter. Do not exaggerate your qualifications, education, or income.

- If you are already interviewing at a company, have had a good informational interview, or have a plan to contact a company on your own, tell the recruiter not to submit your resume to that company. If he submits your resume, you may be at a big disadvantage with other candidates if the company feels that they may owe him a commission (typically between 15% and 25% of your first year's base salary). For this same reason, do not allow your resume to go out without

WORKING WITH 3RD PARTIES AND REFERENCES

knowing the name of the company receiving it, and tell the recruiter not to send your resume to any company without your permission.

- If not really interested in an opportunity, be honest. Don't waste the recruiter's time.

- Most recruiters specialize in an industry. Work only with the ones who specialize in yours and have strong working relationships with employers of interest to you. Check out the recruiter's website and research him in a Google search and on LinkedIn. A good recruiter will have an excellent reputation, understand his client's organization very well, have worked with professionals similar to you in the past, and should know almost immediately if you are a potentially good fit.

- Follow up with the recruiter to get the status of a specific opportunity, but do not call him more than once per week or he may get annoyed and you may appear desperate. Don't be surprised if he doesn't remember you immediately. Recruiters speak with lots of people every day.

- Treat the recruiter in exactly the same way you would treat a corporate recruiter who works for the company directly. Remain professional at all times, proofread your written communications to him, and do not share negative information or doubts about your ability to meet less important job qualifications.

- Work with no more than 3 recruiters, and concentrate on building a strong relationship with the one who appears most interested in working with you.

- Keep your expectations low. Assume that nothing will happen, and you will not be discouraged when he doesn't get back to you. Remember, he will only put his best candidates forward.

> - Don't contact the recruiter's client directly at any time since it will be seen as very unprofessional and will almost certainly disqualify you from the job.
>
> - A good recruiter will schedule and prepare you for interviews, provide you with timely feedback, and work out your compensation and benefits if you are offered the job.

References

Before making the job offer, a company may ask for personal and professional references. When giving a reference, be sure to include the reference's name, position, company, location, phone number, relationship, but **do not include the information on your resume**, since you will need to control these references by getting to them before the employer and suggesting to them what they might say if they are called.

When they are called, you will want them to reinforce the skills, strengths, knowledge and experience that the employer showed the most interest in when he interviewed you. When contacting your references, give them a job description, and offer to email them a copy of the job posting.

> Subj: Job Reference
> Paul, I gave you as a reference for a Financial Analyst job at Steinfeld Industries (job description attached). They were very interested in my problem solving skills, so if you would say something about my performance in that area when they contact you, it might be especially helpful.
> Thanks very much.
> Best Regards,
> Lucy

WORKING WITH 3RD PARTIES AND REFERENCES

If the employer asks for a letter of reference, you can write one for one of your best references to sign if he requests that you do so. If necessary, you can give him a reference letter such as the one below as a sample. **Notice that her contribution to the company is very specific.**

Reference Letter Sample

Dear Mr Jones,

It is my pleasure to recommend Lucy Cameron. Her performance working as a marketing analyst for ABC Company proved to me that she would be a valuable addition to any company.

I was Lucy's direct supervisor during the period of her employment. She worked for me on various projects, including weekly web analytics and marketing performance reporting, and an affiliate marketing program. The quality of her work often exceeded our expectations.

I was also greatly impressed by Lucy's contribution to the team. When the team needed to determine an affiliate marketing strategy, she volunteered to help create a LinkShare report analysis; and contributed very helpful insights and suggestions in a very well designed presentation

If I can be of any further assistance, or provide you with any further information, please do not hesitate to contact me at steven@abccompany.com or 555-555-5555.

Sincerely,

Steven Steinfeld

Digital Marketing Manager

ABC Company

Negotiating Like a Pro

"Negotiation assumes parties are more anxious to agree than to disagree."

— Dean Acheson, Former U.S. Secretary of State

If you have been in transition for an extended period of time, I totally understand that you may ignore the process described in this chapter, and immediately accept a job offer without trying to negotiate an increased level of compensation. However, even in that case, I would suggest that you at least ask the employer, "Is there any flexibility in your salary offer?" before accepting it. If the employer asks, "What did you have in mind?" you might respond with, "I was hoping for a slightly higher base salary." If he is concerned about your satisfaction with the offer, you might hear, "Let me see what I can do," in which case, you have increased your income with very little effort and virtually no risk. If he says, "That's not possible," to your question, you will at least have the satisfaction of having tried.

For all other professional job seekers, know that negotiation is expected, particularly with certain jobs such as sales and customer service, and the potential employer will think more highly of you if you negotiate well. Most job seekers do a poor job of negotiating for 3 major reasons: they do not understand how to value their worth, they are desperate not to screw up the offer (especially in a tough economy), or they feel the need to prove their worth before asking for what they are truly worth (for unknown reasons, women fall into this trap more often than men).

Understanding Your Worth

There are websites (salary.com, payscale.com, bls.gov, glassdoor.com, vault.com, indeed.com) that can give you an idea of salary trends and the salary range for a specific job in a specific area. **Check at least two of these sites BEFORE you go into the first interview.**

If you are asked during the interview process to name a number, it is because they do not want to waste time if you are completely out of the ballpark. Give a wide-range based upon your research, while all the while staying aware of your own salary needs and expectations. Keep in mind that your salary history is really not relevant since the job and company are not exact matches with your last job, and you may have been underpaid in the past (especially if you were with your last company for a very long time). In the end, you may not receive everything you want, but you should also not feel undervalued.

Be aware that if you give a salary number first, the higher the amount that you propose, the higher the amount that will be on the table—but the more risk that you will be screened out. The way to mitigate the risk is to allow the employer to give a number first, but that may lower the number on the table. You will need to make a decision in advance. Do you go first and give a high number or do you allow them to go first with a lower number? The answer may depend on how badly you need the job and how well you understand your potential value to that company.

Large employers extend offers of salary based upon an established range for that position. If they go first, they will often start with an offer that is somewhere below the midpoint, while keeping some room open for negotiation. For example, if the range for a position is $65,000 to $80,000, they will probably make an offer in the vicinity of $70,000 if you have solid experience. **Your goal should be to get above the midpoint** (in this case $72,500).

When they make you that $70,000 offer, take a long pause, followed by, "Thank you for the offer. I'm excited about the opportunity, and would be honored to be part of the company. I was however expecting an offer about 10% higher. In any event, I would like a day to think the offer over. In the meantime, maybe you could find out if there is any flexibility on the base salary." When you talk again the next day, start with, "Did you have a chance to review the base salary since we spoke yesterday?" There is a decent chance that they will have decided to up their offer by something, maybe meeting you half-way ($73,500 in this example since it is half way between the $70K offer and the $77K requested). Not only will this put $3,500 in your pocket within the next 12 months, it will compound with every salary increase (as will the value of any related benefits).

If they wind up offering you anything less than what you requested, ask politely about other ways to reach your compensation goals, "I can live with the base salary that you are offering, but could put our heads together and find a way to get closer to my overall compensation needs?" followed closely by, "For example, would it be possible to have a salary review in six months or would you consider a bonus arrangement for outstanding work?" You might also ask about receiving an extra week of vacation time, especially if they are offering fewer weeks of vacation than you had at your last company.

It's important to remember that if you are being offered the job, you are their first choice. **Trust that they will not risk losing you for a reasonable increase if you keep it friendly and are not obnoxious, intransient or demanding (with some increase being almost guaranteed if you have come to them by way of a referral).** If they still hold tight to their compensation offer and show no flexibility in negotiation, and you feel that you can live with the offer, take it! At least you will know that you received the best deal possible.

Before Accepting the Job

Complete Your Research

If you haven't completed your research online, or had informational interviews at the company, do it now. You may spot a red flag.

Look at the Whole Picture

Keep in mind that salary isn't the only factor you should consider. Are there medical benefits? When will you be eligible for a 401(k) or another retirement plan? Can you expect a performance bonus? How often will you get a salary review? How much vacation time will you receive? Are they offering stock options or profit sharing? Will they allow you to work a certain number of days from home if you have a long commute? How much will you be traveling? What will be your scope of responsibility? What's the reputation of the organization and your new boss? Will you have an opportunity to make a real impact? Can you live with negative aspects of the culture (autocratic, poor work/life balance)? The list goes on. Get the answers to all of your important questions before you accept the offer, even if you are delighted with the base salary.

Long-term Unemployment

"Nothing in the world can take the place of persistence. Persistence and determination alone are omnipotent."

– Calvin Coolidge

Although it is no longer unusual to be unemployed for more than six months, it is considered long term unemployment, and you may be facing a growing and unfair bias against hiring from within this group. However, it is more likely that you have not been applying to the *right* jobs, effectively communicating your value, or adequately explaining what you have been doing since losing your last position.

Between the ages of 40 and 55, you may be considered expensive in an environment where the job may theoretically be done for less money through outsourcing, offshoring, contract work, or by a less seasoned worker. To overcome this challenge, you will need to **ensure that everything in your toolbox (value statement, resume, cover letter, interviewing skills, references) supports your worth**. However, even if it does, you should stay flexible on compensation. You may need to be willing to initially take up to 20% less than your former compensation in order to land the job, particularly if you are considering changing careers.

Keeping a positive mind-set while in a long term transition is especially critical (I have seen too many talented professionals give up their job search out of repeated disappointment when they could have been successful if they had remained persistent and determined (see the next chapter titled *Job Search from the Inside Out*).

Some ways that you can meet the challenge of long term unemployment are as follows:

Change What You Have Been Doing Unsuccessfully

This sounds easy, but I have had clients who have stopped wasting time sending out loads of resumes and cover letters to concentrate on networking, only to be accosted by their spouses/parents for wasting time or being lazy. If this is your situation, please ask them to read the beginning chapters of this book.

Have a Story to Tell Beyond Job Searching

Telling a prospective employer that you have been spending several months or years looking for work is not an acceptable answer to, "What have you been doing since losing your job?" Instead, you will need to explain how you have been keeping your skills sharp or developing new skills, and keeping up with trends. You will also need to directly or indirectly explain why you have not landed a position over an extended period of time— including the obvious (but usually unspoken) question as to why you have not been hired by another organization.

Have a story that clearly shows that you have stayed active, relevant, and engaged in useful activities. Hopefully, you have been doing some temporary or part-time paid work and/or volunteering. If not, get started immediately. In addition, if you have been engaged in planning for your own business, helping a friend get his business launched or turned around, or successfully dealing with family or health issues, include that in your networking conversations and cover letters. You might add in your networking and interviews that you have had some tempting job offers, but have been holding out for the right job. It's also okay to say that you made mistakes in the job search process. In this last case, make sure that you get across what you have learned from your mistakes.

Focus on Networking and Referrals

Rather than concentrate on sending out hundreds more resumes, concentrate on networking and on getting referrals with a strong recommendation to hiring managers (e.g., "Steven has been in transition for several months, but I know that he has been keeping his skills sharp, and think he would be a great fit for this organization. You would be wise to interview him").

Focus on Growth Industries

These include health care, IT and business services, social work, green energy, and leisure and hospitality. Find out how to get qualified for consideration through informational interviews.

Learn Something New

There is a reasonable chance that your next job will require new skills ("upskilling"). Don't procrastinate acquiring these new skills because you feel that it will take too much time. If you do, a year from now (by which time you might have already closed the skills gap), you might be wishing you had started sooner. Don't get started on additional education or training before determining the right job by completing the Discovery phase of your job search. Find out what new knowledge or skills are necessary to compete effectively for your next job. The last thing you need is to accrue an education or training expense that will not get you closer to the right job. Get back in the game also by reading, attending conferences, informational interviews, and volunteering. Also check out on-line courses (www.usnews.com/education/online-education), including those that may be given for free (http://www.coursera.org).

Volunteer

See the chapter titled *Volunteer Strategically*.

Find Employers That Seek Out Seasoned Professionals

If you are an older professional, research companies that actually seek out seasoned employees. Check out websites (AARP) that lists the names of these employers.

Consider Contacting Former Employers

If you've maintained good relationships with former employers, why not go to them to see if they have any openings? You already have the connections to get your foot in the door, so make the most of them.

Take a Hard Look at Small Companies and Start-Ups

Some of these may be particularly in need of your business and industry experience, and the personal strengths that can only come from maturity.

Once you get beyond age 55, you should be flexible and open to all options since many companies may be concerned about the cost of your health care and/or your interest in staying long-term. These options include part-time and temporary work, consulting or contract work, and opening your own small business.

Part-Time Work

I am not referring to being underemployed. I am talking about working your way from part-time work into full time work (which requires that your part-time work is in the "right" company with the "right" job in sight), or a "portfolio career" in which you string together two or three part-time jobs into a single career. An example of a portfolio career would be an accountant who does part-time bookkeeping for a company, teaches accounting as an adjunct professor at a local college, and does seasonal tax preparation work.

Temporary Work

Temporary work is the fastest growing job category. It should be entered into with the idea of turning it into full time work by going above and beyond what is expected, and by developing a friendly relationship with your supervisor. If it cannot realistically turn into the *right* job, it should be entered into without slowing down the primary job search process more than absolutely necessary. If you need a job urgently, when applying for a highly competitive full time job, consider telling the employer that you are willing to start on a temporary basis. This may give you a leg up on workers who are unwilling to accept this kind of employment.

Consulting or Contract Work

Consulting or contract work can offer great flexibility, interesting challenges and exceptional learning experiences. However, before you accept consulting or other contract work, take a minute to consider if the particular project will add to your resume, provide networking opportunities, and result in new expertise that will improve your future project or long term work prospects. If you have consulting or contract type skills, but prefer to work more independently and with greater flexibility as a freelancer, check out opportunities at www.3desk.com.

Changing Careers

It's easy to say that you should transfer your skills from one career to another, but in a highly competitive job market, employers feel that they have the option to look for the perfect or near perfect candidate. The perfect candidate is the one who matches up exactly with the criteria set out for the job (number of years of overall experience, experience in a specific industry sector, previously holding the same job level). **Avoid HR and go straight to the hiring manager.** This is always the preferred approach, but critical when you do not line up exceptionally well with the specific background requirements laid out in the official job description. If you do decide to change careers, you are likely to be more successful if you commit to leaving your last career behind while committing 100% to your new career.

Opening a Small Business

Keep in mind that there are 3 options to opening your own business: starting it from scratch, buying an existing business, or franchising. These options are beyond the scope of this book, but I do offer the following advice: Do not consider opening a small business without a solid business plan and experienced legal and accounting support. One way to test the validity of your plans is to contact your local chapter of SCORE (www.score.org) for a free mentoring and business plan review. They also offer low cost seminars on subjects such as marketing and accounting.

The good news is that with effective tools, strategies, and healthy doses of persistence and aggressiveness, even the longest-term job seeker will successfully return to the job market.

Job Search from the Inside Out

"If you think you can or you think you can't, you are probably right."

— Henry Ford

A successful job search does not start by looking outward for new opportunities, but with looking inward at your current level of fear, anxiety, and motivation. **No matter how strong your resume or skill set, you will be challenged to put the focus, energy and confidence you need to successfully implement what you have learned from this book without the proper mind-set.**

Mind-set includes beliefs and assumptions that lead us to making certain decisions. Sometimes these are self-defeating. For example, if you assume that no one hires around the Christmas holidays, you will probably slow down your job search in December. On the other hand, it you believe that hiring during the holidays is strong, you have a good chance of changing your experience and your outcome (December is actually one of the best months to job search since hiring is strong for many companies going into a new fiscal year in January).

The 2013 report from *Career Thought Leader Job Seeker Success Survey* lists the following key elements in keeping a positive mind-set:

- Optimistic Self-Talk. Do not question your self-worth when the job search process frustrates you (e.g., you do not get a response to your resume or you do not get the job after an excellent interview).

- Empowering Actions. Embrace the job search process, and take action. Taking action helps to bring clarity to what you need to do. Engage in activities that provide mastery and/or accomplishment and keep focused.

- Disempowering Self-Talk. Do not focus on your weaknesses or worst case scenarios ("I will never get a job"). Challenge less rational thoughts or picture yourself floating above them.

- Disempowering Actions. Do not slow or stop your search. Discouragement can come on very quickly, but once it takes hold, it leaves very slowly. Keep thinking about how exciting it will be when you finally land that great job.

- The Most Effective Job Search Activity is networking, followed by generally improving your job search skills (the purpose of this book).

15 Tips for Improving Mind-set and Resilience

Start with one. Remember that it takes about 21 days to establish a new habit.

1. Start the day with 20 sips of water to get energized from the inside out

2. Avoid watching or listening to the news to start the day. Instead, start the day with quiet time to get in touch with your frame of mind. Follow with some energizing music.

JOB SEARCH FROM THE INSIDE OUT

3. Give yourself some downtime from job search. Take a slow walk or a long shower, or even daydream, to stir creative and constructive ideas.

4. If you are a seasoned professional, do not use words or phrases that allow you to think of yourself as old, such as "I had a senior moment."

5. Put in 15 minutes per day in physical activity such as walking or gardening.

6. Pursue things that you love to do. Do at least one thing every day that makes you happy.

7. Connect with family, friends, and community, including spending time working out of the local coffee shop).

8. Continue to learn and grow every day, especially in your career field.

9. Avoid procrastination. Break down daunting tasks into manageable bite-sized pieces, set up a system of rewards, and prioritize activities into A, B, and C categories (making sure you get to the A's each day).

10. Avoid anyone with a negative mind-set. This includes your uncle Charlie who corners you at Thanksgiving dinner, "Steven, Did I hear that you are still out of work? I was laid off 20 years ago on a Friday and had a new job by Monday."

11. Consciously smile at other people 3 times per day.

12. Send a positive email to someone in your social network or post a positive online message (e.g., on Facebook).

13. Write 3 positive things that happened during the day, plus one small detail of one of your greatest work accomplishments.

14. Tap your competitive spirit by understanding and reminding yourself that someone less qualified than you will be getting your *right* job if you don't get more proactive.

15. View transition as an opportunity to get into a more rewarding career or job than the last job, or series of jobs, that you may have struggled through. Visualize how great it is going to feel on the first day of work at **YOUR BEST JOB EVER!**

About the Author

Steven Steinfeld is a professional job search coach, speaker and author. He brings his career and job search coaching techniques to executives and professionals, MBA programs and international students through his acclaimed workshops and books. Steven's innovative approaches have resulted in TV, newspaper and radio interviews on current hiring trends, overcoming the challenges of long-term unemployment and ageism, as well as the importance of positive mind-set during career and job transition. His LinkedIn profile is in the top 1% viewed and he currently has about 600 LinkedIn Endorsements.

Steven's seminars and workshops have been sponsored by more than a dozen university alumni programs and local and national career centers and networking organizations, and he is on staff at the business schools at Northern Illinois University and the Illinois Institute of Technology. He is also on the Advisory Boards of Consult-Global, The Careers College and InternshipDesk, and has consulted with the Associated Colleges of Illinois.

Steven is also the founder at Executive to Executive Coaching, Inc., a network of coaches working with senior leadership to maximize personal and organizational achievement, transition and transformation.

Prior to becoming a career, job search, and executive coach, Steven had a distinguished career in senior management and business consulting at global technology organizations, and led multi-cultural sales and marketing teams in more than 20 countries on six continents. He brings much of his expertise in sales, marketing, and strategic planning and the experience gained in hundreds of hiring decisions, to his work.

He holds a degree in Psychology from CUNY and Certification in Marketing Management from The Wharton School of the University of Pennsylvania.

Steven has been honored for his service to the community. His volunteer organizations have included: The Career Transitions Center of Chicago, Career Advancement Network, Access Living, and The Executive Service Corp of Chicago.

Please connect with Steven and email him your questions
www.linkedin/in/stevensteinfeld
www.stevensteinfeld.com
steven@stevensteinfeld.com

Made in the USA
Charleston, SC
13 July 2014